HOOPS OF FIRE

Hoops of Fire

FIFTY YEARS OF FICTION BY PAKISTANI WOMEN

Edited by

Aamer Hussein

Saqi Books

Cover photograph: Mumtaz Shirin, *circa* 1947

British Library Cataloguing-in-Publication Data
A catalogue record for this book is available from the
British Library

ISBN 0 86356 039 3 (pbk)

This edition first published 1999

Saqi Books
26 Westbourne Grove
London W2 5RH

Contents

Foreword

In the period following the partition of the Indian subcontinent in 1947, Urdu literature in Pakistan has developed a dynamic identity of its own. It retains, on the one hand, sociolinguistic links with Urdu literature in India, and reflects, on the other, the demands and vagaries of a new chapter of history that is in the process of being transcribed. It raises interesting questions of autonomous cultural identity and the ever-evolving relationship of art with politics. Contemporary Pakistani literature also reveals fascinating parallels with the literature of other nascent post-colonial societies and engages fearlessly with the genres and modes produced in the 'developed' countries of the West, redefining and reconstructing them to its own purposes.

Urdu literature has yet, however, to be accorded its rightful place in the annals of world literature. The South Asian writers who have recently gained renown in the West are all Anglophone and are usually subsumed under the Indo-Anglian label. With a handful of honourable exceptions, those writers who have been translated from national/regional languages have been relegated to the confined space of academic journals. For all the lip-service paid to their achievements, the space given to women writers is negligible, particularly when one considers the major contribution they have made to experiments in form and subject over the last half-century, equalling and often surpassing their male contemporaries.

It was not my original intention to produce an anthology devoted exclusively to women, but my publishers rightly pointed out the gap and my own readings in Urdu fiction served to confirm the decision: too much writing by women has suffered neglect over the past half-century. *We Sinful Women*, Rukhsana Ahmad's pioneering anthology of contemporary feminist poets in translation, introduced Pakistan's women poets to an Anglophone audience; in the present book, an anthology of short fiction translated from the Urdu, I make an attempt to redress the balance by presenting a number of prominent and lesser-known women writers of short fiction. Their stories are accessible and yet often challenging in form; in content, they are at once universal and deeply rooted in the particular experience of a nation and its psyche.

A theme emerges, perhaps: that of the effect of the first forty years of the country's history – from partition until and after the death of Bhutto – on the imagination of its women. Though purely subjective experience is also in evidence here, those writers who traffic less in political and more in personal experience have nevertheless been liberated into writing by the politically conscious writings of the first wave of literary women. Their dream worlds are illuminated and darkened by the vagaries and vicissitudes of the society that shapes them. Fahmida Riaz's Amina, exiled in India, sees her alienation in sociohistorical terms: she writes 'a number of passionate poems, exposing the gaping flaws in a democratic system that still allowed for horrifying poverty'. Khalida Husain's nameless narrator in the title story moves in a metaphysical darkness: 'And am I not answerable to that world, beyond the Third World, that lives within me?' Yet their wistful loneliness is identical.

Several stories, translated especially for this selection, appear here for the first time in English; others have previously been available only in Pakistan. I hope they serve to urge other editors and translators to make their much-needed contribution to the field of translating contemporary Pakistani fiction. This is particularly relevant, as Pakistan is now half a century old. Its fictions are the literary mirror of a turbulent history and the partition of a language; its women writers, always an equal force in this culture, have not only been vital contributors to the art of fiction, but have often renovated and even subverted its prevalent discourses.

The major Urdu writers, and indeed its emerging young writers who have as yet to secure their reputation, contribute much to an international debate that seeks to decentralize Eurocentric aesthetic theories and notions. Several of the authors included in the anthology are also novelists, but the short story has a place in South Asian literature second only to poetry, and Urdu writers have almost without exception showed great mastery of the shorter forms: the story, the tale and the novella. Handling with equal ease the romantic and unrealistic modes inherited from past tradition, European realism, Marxist-inspired protest writing and the postmodernist strategies characteristic of our century, they have demonstrated that the development of fictional techniques is, in spite of ongoing ideological debate, not so much a question of conflict or opposition between realism and fantasy, tradition and modernity or art and politics, but an often contradictory juxtaposition of opposites in an imaginative and linguistic crucible. Modern Urdu literature, widely held to be descended from the edicts of the socially orientated Progressive Writers Movement, has nevertheless retained its links with indigenous pre-novelistic modes, and it is this coexistence of apparently irreconcilable elements that modern writers have creatively exploited.

Although the anthology focuses largely on writings from the 1960s to the 1980s, the pieces by the two writers here who rose to prominence earlier – Mumtaz Shirin and Khadija Mastoor – effectively illustrate the two dominant tendencies, respectively the aesthetic-fabulist and the social realist, yet each displays traces of the antithetical tendency in her work. Mumtaz Shirin's piece is an early monologue, written while she was still in her teens, which shows at once her modernist aesthetic and her understanding of women's need for self-expression. Khadija Mastoor, as a feminist, focused with brilliance on the lives of dispossessed women, and her story here,

Godfather, mirrors her preoccupations. Women of the underclasses are often her central characters and though her stories are in method ostensibly realistic, poetic diction and picaresque situations link her work to older narrative modes. This section also includes one of the stories of the doyenne of Pakistani fiction, Hijab Imtiaz Ali.

Mastoor and Shirin belonged to the generation of Ismat Chughtai, who chose to remain in India at partition, and Qurratulain Hyder, who migrated to Pakistan at partition but later returned to India. Hyder left an enormous gap in the world of Pakistani literature, but her influence is everywhere. Also from this generation of trail-blazing women writers are Jamila Hashmi and Altaf Fatima, who can be called the inheritors of Hyder's mantle. Hashmi was in the forefront of women's writing in the 1960s and insisted on giving equal space in her fiction to Hindus, Sikhs and Muslims, stressing a common cultural experience. Her radical feminism is often refracted through the perspectives of male narrators, through whom she incorporates in her stories a critique of patriarchal norms, thus raising burning questions about class and gender. Arguably – and perhaps, in the Pakistani context, unusually – a better novelist than she is a short-story writer, Hashmi is represented here by her famous story of rape and exile in the wake of partition, *Exile*. This is one of my favourite stories in any language and combines, in my opinion, the sociohistorical canvas and the sweep of her novels with the subjectivity of modernist short fiction and the lyric intensity of a traditional ballad.

Altaf Fatima, who belongs to the generation of Hashmi and Mastoor and is also a fine novelist, has in the last decade displayed an excellence in the short-story form that places her in the first rank of Pakistan's writers. Her story here combines traditional narrative and postmodern polyphony with an overlay of political protest to tell the tale of a peasant woman's seduction and betrayal by a Western anthropologist.

The next generation of writers, who were born around the 1930s and 1940s, often disclaim 'national' or local influence and identify with Camus, Kafka, Marquez and Kundera. However, they have all inherited a passion for indigenous myth and parable and tend to present even their most political statements in a framework of fable and poetry. Since several of these writers are from the Punjab, they have introduced a strong local and rural flavour to the Urdu language, using it to depict a recognizably Pakistani landscape rather than the elegant, urbanized northern India so often evoked by the earlier generation. Partition also figures far less in their work; their metaphors and tropes usually represent current concerns such as military oppression, patriarchal and feudal norms, sexuality and gender discrimination.

Included here are Farkhanda Lodhi, Razia Fasih Ahmed, Umme Amara and Khalida Husain. The latter is often considered to be this generation's finest exponent of the short story; she locates the perspective of urban women in a semi-fantastic but recognizably Pakistani landscape, and creates new legends that articulate the social and political preoccupations of a new age in a tone that simultaneously evokes ancient bards, epic poets, Kafka, Camus and Woolf. The title story has been chosen from her work. Fasih Ahmed, who won a major literary prize in the mid-1960s with her novel *Abla Pa* [Footsore], is notable, above all, for the emphasis her novels place on the lives of confident, middle-class women struggling to maintain their autonomy in a society riddled with moribund patriarchal strictures. She has also used the conventions of Western modernism – Faulknerian multiple narrators, for example – in her readable, popular novels. Lodhi, on the other hand, can be seen as the natural successor to Mastoor; her fiction, however, reflects her Punjabi roots in its robust diction and folksy settings. Umme Amara's study of the 1971 war for Bangladesh completes this section. Reading these writers is a fascinating exercise in comparative criticism with any equivalent movement from Latin America, Eastern Europe, or the Far or Middle East.

   In the range of their preoccupations and experimentation, writers born around partition and after equal much Anglophone writing from any continent, and are possibly closer in spirit to the writings of Assia Djebar or Hoda Barakat. To complete the collection we have two of these: the trail-blazing poet Fahmida Riaz, who has recently turned to writing fiction and is one of the country's finest writers in any genre – her bold, highly political stories defy generic classifications; and Azra Abbas, who writes both poetry and prose. These writers effectively display the influence of their predecessors, both Eastern and Western; they maintain a careful balance between the continuation of a thriving literary tradition and the changes of strategy demanded by the state of continuous flux in which they live.

Aamer Hussein
November 1997

Azra Abbas

Voyages of Sleep

1

The feet walking on water were ours indeed
   And you desired to touch the rustling clothes –
   Are your fingertips stained with our rosy colours?
   Do you know that butterflies are looking for the very same
colours? But you mustn't touch them – they will fly off with those
colours and our feet, walking on water, will see them fly but won't be
able to stop.
   But will those feet be ours?
   Because then, sitting by our mothers' sides, we would be stitching
clothes and a spicy, dust-coloured odour would be emanating from
kitchens.

Is it true that in days to come, scorching on the other side of the sun,
our bodies will account for their sins and birds will fly off with our
eyes hidden in their feathers?
   Is this true?

But now our hands are fragrant with words more powerful than love
and we get up from our beds at night, for our bangles start jingling by
themselves and the soft light from our arms flows afar as fragrance.

So where do we wander to?
O lights, following us in the dark!

Why, in the desire to walk on open waters, are we always given to the immobility of our abodes? Where, far away from us, are our dreams rejoicing? Why has the bright evening form estranged us?

2

Pillows lie on empty beds like forlorn girls. Music, bustling with the wind, sinking into the flesh, the sky looking for water, people returning home – far, faraway heads droop with heavy dreams – a cold water stream runs through our bosoms and white birds fly about with water in their beaks, pairs of pigeons chase each other, ships anchor on shores and someone lightly touches the shoulder.

Virgin blood! You'll return from those shores as sunshine has spread over half the oceans and flowing footsteps have taken up cramped journeys – give away the eyes panting around loneliness and the miseries of the journey to the senseless path.

Far away, among dense, white-flowered trees, sounds of footsteps do not look back for opulent oceans – here, journeys are soundless and dream-forms, like pounded cotton, pass away unendowed.

Sufferings of the night increase in diminishing light and desires can be heard like the hooves of horses on flat, even roads – we have no clue of days to come – countless staring eyes, like black rocks climbing down dark trees, move toward the oceans and bodies are half-burnt in the half-spread light of the sun – outside the whirl of trees, shadows of winds, sounds and moments go on extending, and skies, unable to bear this are closing in.

Prayers, escaping from the palms, are now part of the imperceptible air.

3

Picking shells from raw earthen walls, staying awake with the night, inscribing their impressions upon dark, stormy, fate-chasing winds, lips loaded with prayers – and in the quietness of burning afternoons, like the sweetness of a love-laden name, our maidenhood.

And O God!

This forest, accompanying us like an invisible shadow, leaves its naked songs in our bodies and resembles people who quench their thirst from snake-filled ponds.

Eyes of a frightened sparrow, broken wings, with innumerable flightless fears and the first utterance of a homeless, newborn babe, like heavenly rains, create words that permeate the lips with the fragrance of chaste prayers.

Before dusk, the desire for a journey that impairs the joints, heels submitting to travel and weightless moments burdening the body persist within us, but night demands accountability for its loneliness and breaking away from the unseen sky, to endure the suffering of hapless days, we free ourselves.

Where is the wakeful eye grieving the half-moon and where is the vision not bound by dreams?

Where is it all that's in the darkness?

O light of time – sifting through songs of moments, just a sip's thirst!

Where is it all
That's in the darkness?

Translated by Yasmin Hameed

Altaf Fatima

When the Walls Weep

Horse-drawn carriages are gradually being eased off the streets of Lahore (newspaper headline)

Wild animals are a national resource: it is our duty to protect them (poster on a wall)

And the wall says: I am not that wall the builder made with the help of a mixture of mud, cement and concrete. I am that wall made by the sun and the moon which human beings call the beautiful hills of Margalla. And I wish I could show the poster to the owner of the black Mercedes that knocked down a child sitting behind his brother on a scooter very near a school, crushed him and drove away.

And what of that other child, the one I must travel so far to find? Perhaps he is waiting for me.

But he doesn't even know that we're going to get him. It doesn't matter. His blue eyes, his jute-blonde hair . . . He must be very lonely there, and unhappy.

The story that Gul Bibi told the villagers is the one I watched, scene by scene, for six months. But I swear by the dark night that I have not heard a word of it until today, though I have it all on tape within me, from start to finish, and in her own words.

Who? What? When? Why?

She herself will answer all your questions.

You only have to bear in mind that she's a woman – a woman of the valley, at that. And all valley women – never mind which valley, Kashmir, Kaghan or Kalash – remind one of ripe apples hanging from boughs on the trees of their gardens.

The characters of this story are all central: there are no extras. This is more or less the sequence in which they appear, according to the plot. A widow whose winsome daughter has just been wed. A blonde, blue-eyed foreign woman. And a blonde, blue-eyed tourist – or if you want to discard the cliché you could call him a research scholar, a student of anthropology – well, let's continue, just listen to the tape.

— Someone in the bazaar had told me that a job was available in the Rest House. A foreign lady had just arrived. She needed a servant. I was starving. I lived near the mosque by the corner of the bazaar in my shack made of sticks and thatch. After marrying off my Mahgul I lay among my baskets like a rotten apple. When Mahgul left her, uncle stopped sending me money for my expenses, and I was starving. I went along as soon as I heard about the job and started work straight away. But the woman seemed a bit mad to me. Eccentric. She'd write all night with her light on, then fall asleep, wake up suddenly and stalk around her room. She'd be putting paper in her typewriter before the first call to prayer and I'd hear her tapping away. Then she'd wake me up, calling, Gul Bibi, get me some coffee. I couldn't stand this habit of hers. During the day she'd go off into the woods to collect herbs, roots, leaves. Once she asks me, Gul Bibi, she says, does any one practise white magic in your village? I'd been wondering about her for a while, anyway. These are devilish practices, I tell her clearly, we Muslims don't play around with magic. If our own herbs and poultices don't work, we go down to some holy man for an amulet. And we don't even have a holy man in our village. After that, I started to watch her. At night she'd take off all her clothes and stare at her naked body in the mirror. She'd go on staring and then begin to weep. But without a sound. Strange. Mahgul's youth had taken mine away and the sight of this woman's was bringing it back. I thought her spells must be working on me. But I had to feed myself somehow, after all. She was a good woman, though, just kept on writing, tapping away, then one day she'd go off to town with a stack of those papers of hers. She wouldn't come back for days.

The tape breaks off at this point.

This is when he appears, in his blue jeans and checked shirt under his Peshawari fur jacket, his Swati hat and his backpack and his camera. And settles in the Rest House. (Wait . . . I've sorted out the sequence of the tapes again. Just let me adjust the sound a bit . . .)

— He settled in so comfortably that I just assumed he was her man. I hardly needed to ask her about that. She'd spend whole days in the woods, gathering her sticks. And he, perched for hours on the white rocks by the Naran, would bait the trout hiding in its waters. He'd trap about a seer of trout a day . . . (Stop. When my boys tried to catch some trout in the Naran they were stopped by a guard. Who created a great fuss. And we thought, well, if we can't have trout, we'll have some corn on the cob instead. It's so sweet, so succulent here. Grains of corn, fields of maize . . . thoughts, like a top, spinning here and there, at the gates of schools, around hours of play, horses, silence, seed-pearls . . . And a child with eyes as light and clear as the waters of the Naran and hair as bright as sheaves of corn waiting, waiting . . . For whom? For me, perhaps . . .) Cut! The button of the tape recorder's been switched on again. Automatically – or by demonic interference? The voice: a man in the bazaar.

— After the foreign lady left, the man that Gul Bibi had taken for her lover stayed on for another week. And then one day with his pack and his camera on his shoulder, he strolled up to the Rest House's cook on his long legs and told him to give Gul Bibi her mistress's keys when she got back.

— I saw him go off on the Kaghan bus. Gul Bibi was ill that day. She lay on her bed in her shack all day, with her scarf over her face. When I gave her the key the next day she couldn't believe it. She went on repeating to the mullah, the gentleman shouldn't have done that, he shouldn't have left the lady's keys with Gul Khan. Who knows what he's walked off with . . .

— She didn't even know his name. Twenty days went by since he'd left, then thirty. The lady hadn't come back yet. Gul Bibi hadn't been properly paid, and since she wasn't working, how could she claim a salary? These foreigners ask you to account for every penny you claim. Then one day no one saw Gul Bibi all day. The door of her house, too, was locked. When even the last bus to Kaghan had gone, a ten-year-old boy called Sultan brought a message to Gul Bibi's daughter: Your mother has married Shakoor. She's left with him on the last bus for Batrasi. Shakoor has found work in the forest there. This key belongs to the foreign lady. Give it back to her when she returns.

— The message amazed everyone. There was no man by that name in our village. Another thirty days went by; someone said they'd seen the foreign lady at the bus terminal with her luggage. I thought of telling her where she could find her key, but she went straight from the bus to Gul Bibi's daughter's house to get it. That, too, amazed us.

The next voice, soft, tiny. Maria's.

— I met her at the Balakot lorry depot. She had henna on her hands and her wrists were full of bangles. She was dressed in flowered chintz and the ribbon of her braid was decorated with little bells. She looked pregnant to me. Her eyes lit up when I teased her about it. Then she told me herself that she'd left my key with her daughter. I'll have to look for another woman to help me out now: I'm meant to stay on for another two months. (The voice begins to fade. A long sigh.) I wouldn't have expected this of you . . . John?

Cut.

The voice of the man from the bazaar again.

— It all lasted exactly five months. I've counted on my fingers. Autumn has begun. The desert wind is pregnant with snow. That's how it was then, the weather, when she got off at the lorry depot one day. She was dressed in black, her wrists were bare, her face desolate, her hair dishevelled and her belly like a barrel. She floated along like a bubble to the house of her daughter, who was standing at the door with a dish of flour in her hands. She fell into her arms and began to weep and wail. We all had to point out to her that she should have some concern for her daughter's condition. We tore her away, with difficulty. When we asked her what the trouble was, she said that Shakoor had done battle with jinns in the jungle and the conflict had killed him. The jinns didn't even spare his corpse; they spirited it away.

— What will be, will be, we said; in all events you have to thank the Creator . . .

The tape suddenly winds to its end and snaps off. Because I had fallen asleep. I always feel sleepy when I'm worried. When I went to the office earlier today the newspapers had arrived and quite by mistake I picked them up. Boom. Boom. On every side the stench of burning flesh. The smell of dust risen from fallen houses and buildings. Tanks. The reek of rotting corpses. God, how these newspapermen exaggerate. Here in a place like Naran you can't even believe what you read. Lord, you made the earth so beautiful and people's hearts so . . . where do I go now, so full of fury? I'm not going back. I'll lose myself here, in this beauty. The boys tremble: but school opens soon, they say. You can't spend your life grieving over everyone's sorrows. And I haven't even reached the place where the child with blue eyes and hair like corn . . .

So. The account of his birth.

And this is the testimony of an aged midwife with twisted hands.

— Maria was always concerned that there wasn't a hospital around here, not even a dispensary. How long can people survive on herbs and roots and incantations? Someone should at least set up a maternity centre. We'd actually taken her for a doctor at first, and we'd land up at her door with our aches and pains and blisters. The poor thing would begin to weep and say in gestures, I'm no doctor, she'd say, but you couldn't expect them to believe her. The result was that she'd be relieved of all the medicines she'd brought along for her own use. This time she'd spoken to all the big shots around and they'd ended up unloading their own woes on her; doctors won't work here, they said, they don't like it, they want to stay on in their big cities where money is good. Maria was left in tears once again.

— I'd say, trying to console her, don't worry, there's always God. Then she took off. And look at the ways of the Lord, mother and daughter delivering their babies at the same time, and I tried to take care of both of them. Both of them gave birth to males. I bathed them and dressed them, and when I took Gul Bibi's son to the mullah and asked him to whisper the name of God in his ear, he panicked and put him down on the ground as if the child were the devil's spawn. What kind of child is this? he roared. Hair like corn and eyes like sapphires. He was terrified. I gestured to him to keep his silence. He's given to us by God, so do your duty and whisper His name in his ear. And when Gul Bibi his mother saw the boy, her smile vanished in tears, and then she quietly died.

— Afzal Khan, Gul Bibi's son-in-law, still asks me every time he catches me alone: Are you sure my mother-in-law gave birth to this child? Then raise your hand in the direction of the Ka'aba and swear that my wife has nothing to do with him.

— And each time I've raised my hand and said: Mahgul's only

connection with the child is that he came from her mother's belly. He's so young, the boy, and the woman whose mother's womb harboured him doesn't have it in her power to protect him, for her husband wakes her up at night and demands: Tell me the truth, is this child really your mother's, or did the midwife place him by your mother's side in the middle of the night just to protect you? If that's the story, then I swear by God I'm going to shoot him with this bullet. And he shows her the bullet and says: So that . . . so that . . . he can never again play such games with someone else's life. That's why Mahgul begged Janet, who was leaving the place after a long sojourn there, Madam, she said, take him away with you, since Mother died I've even been afraid to give him a piece of bread, he doesn't have a well-wisher or a protector.

Yes, Mahgul, he isn't a trout, he doesn't belong to a protected species. So you have to be patient. We both have to be patient. And wait for the time when . . .

In my distress, I've come out here, to the bazaar. On the slope leading down to it is a mosque made of wood, from which I can hear the muezzin's (unamplified) voice. He never sings before or after the call to prayer, but just now he's reading aloud from the Quran. And when the woman who was buried alive is asked: What was the crime for which you were executed – what then?

> That will be the hour when
> The sun will be enveloped
> And the stars will lose their light
> And mountains will walk
> And the seas will become flames
> And the book of reckoning will be opened
> And the skin of the skies will be ripped away
> And all, in this hour of revelation, will be revealed.

And watching all this the walls of a city weep, and within me the walls

of my being are drenched in the drizzle of my silent weeping.
And bright letters proclaim on the hills of Margalla:

WILD ANIMALS ARE A NATIONAL RESOURCE! TO PROTECT THEM IS OUR DUTY!

Translated and abridged by Aamer Hussein

Khadija Mastoor

Godfather

The hideous midnight silence seemed to whisper a murderous plot. And Godfather walked with assurance down the middle of the tarmacked street as if it was made just for her. Guardian sentries whistled, somewhere nearby. A strange terror emanated from the menacing silence. Godfather was oblivious to the sounds of the whistles. The metal head of her walking stick ground the tarmac and her heavy, masculine boots made a racket. Despair dripped from her face. She sighed deeply, over and over again, then looked at the sky with weary eyes as if there, too, hung a heavy lock. She was muttering something – swearing or praying, who knows? The sentries were approaching her now but she strode on, step upon balanced step, with the same steadiness. 'Who are you?' The voice was so near, she had to stand still. There was such despair and grief in the way she stood – perhaps she didn't want to stand. The sentry ogled her, amazed. Such a strapping figure of a woman, stick in hand, wearing men's shoes and a big loose shirt, enormous, wide-trousered *shalwar* and no *dupatta*. Godfather remained silent for a moment, watching the gawping soldier, as if to say, 'Brother, let me walk my fill today.' The soldier turned and let out a loud whistle. The sentries' footsteps came nearer. 'Who are you? Are you dumb – is that why you won't speak?' the soldier yelled and his voice smudged into the far distance.

'Why are you bothering me, my man? Get on with your business,' Godfather said quietly.

'Mind my own business, you slag! Tell me, who you are.' The sentry pounced on her.

'I'm your father, you bastard!' She came to life, bashing the pavement with her stick. The fragility of the world seemed to turn into a curse, beating on her face like rain. The sentry hissed an obscenity. 'Come on – to the station. Roaming around at 2.00 in the morning with a truncheon. Slag.'

'You'll take me to the station, will you?' She fell on the soldier. 'Take me to the station. I'll show you: take me to the station.' She dusted his leg with her stick. Then, as he fearfully went for his truncheon, she brought it down on him with such force that she split open his head. Its metal tip scattered his brain around. She was muttering who knows what, under her breath. In the sallow, insipid moonlight, the living, pulsing blood flowed black. The steps of the other sentries sounded close.

Bemused, Godfather saw the blood and her feet lifted, ready to run. She had only gone a few paces when six soldiers surrounded her, divested her of her cane and handcuffed her. Leaving two soldiers to guard the corpse, the other four flanked her, two on each side, and set off for the nearby station. The soldiers spoke about their dead companion and swore at Godfather. But she walked silently, thinking who knows what. And the night seemed to spit with fury like the soldiers.

Godfather was detained at the station for three days. They didn't need to investigate, she'd been in jail several times. They had her entire history. They kept her all those days just to find out why she hated the dead sentry – and to get her lover's address. She insisted she had no lover now, no acquaintances even. But no one believed her and the female jailers gave her a sound thrashing. On the fourth day they put her in an armoured car and transported her to prison where she was shut in a cell until her case was decided.

When Godfather was brought to that solitary cell, she wasn't laughing as usual, calling the cell a lovely house, she didn't tease or joke with the sentries but remained absolutely silent, and when the iron door of her cell was shut, she spread out a mat on the mud platform, placing her head where it had been raised to form a pillow. All day she stared silently at the ceiling. Some watery, split-pea lentils sat in an aluminium pot alongside two coarse, thick *chappatis*, trying to tempt her. At night, they force-fed her. But her demeanour didn't change much. Outside the iron door, guard duty was in progress. The yellow light of the lanterns glimmered from here to there. 'Barrack no. 1, barrack no. 2. Everything's fine, everything's fine,' the female wardens' voices responded to each other. Godfather kept sighing. Perhaps today the memories of her life, begun in a meagre household, had returned, bent on tormenting her.

Perhaps that was what she replayed, lying in the dark, watching something.

Those days when her father worked as a butler in a nearby house and her mother grumbled, eking out the month on fifteen rupees. In those days her name was Kaneez, not Godfather. Fifteen rupees and six lives. She never had a stomachful to eat. So she had become quarrelsome. She never felt the slightest shame in grabbing her four sisters' share of food, to fill her own belly. Mother would chastise her, citing the gratitude and restraint of her sisters, but come mealtimes, she pranced into the kitchen, forgetting all admonitions, and snatched their portions like a monkey. Mother consoled and cosseted her other offspring in their hunger. She cursed Kaneez and wished her evil. Kaneez cried as she watched Mother lavishing her affection on her siblings and, for a bit, withdrew into silence. But when she entered the kitchen she would again leap and prance, in the process smashing several of the clay pots and containers. Mother pounded her breast and once or twice even beat her with sticks of firewood. Yet when the women who lived round about criticized her and called her names, Mother said hopefully that she would grow out of it. But Kaneez's habits deteriorated. Around the age of thirteen, she was confined to purdah but her ways didn't alter a shred. Nor did her father's salary increase. Now she learned new tricks. She spent hours twisting her neck round the door of their servant's quarters and when the women from the grand houses came out dressed in their finery, she'd clap loudly and start shouting:

'I wish to God these eaters of *pulao* and sweet rice would die. I wish to God these wearers of finery would die.' She would stop the travelling vendors of *pakoras* and sweets, then run in without buying anything, provoking their abuse. And one day she surpassed herself. She swore at the wife of her father's employer, cursing her for not increasing his salary. That day, he nearly lost his job. He was ordered to vacate the quarters and it was only by falling at his mistress's feet and begging her to excuse the prating of an immature child that he continued to earn his crust. When Father came home, he flogged her so severely with a stout stick, she couldn't leave her bed for days. After that the door was always locked.

Around fifteen she was, when Mother arranged her marriage, to put her to rights. They borrowed twenty rupees and the preparatory period began. During that time, she didn't fight for food and radiance shone out of her face in spite of a half-empty stomach. Some of her friends had married recently and they told her that quite apart from food and new clothes, a bride receives the kind of love from her husband that no one else can give.

After leaving for her husband's home, Kaneez forgot her past woes. Her husband loved her wholeheartedly and her mother-in-law was so caring that she fed Kaneez with her own hands, noon and night. But when she lifted her bridal veil and wanted to see the house, she realized she was only the mistress in name. The orders came from her horse-toothed mother-in-law. Her husband's twenty-rupee salary was also handed over to his mother. Swiftly, she said farewell to her bridehood and tried to take control of the household. But her mother-in-law turned vicious as a witch. She locked Kaneez out of the room which contained three enormous tin trunks, banned her from so much as peeping into the kitchen and wouldn't let her touch a penny of her husband's salary. That apart, she denied her the delicious titbits that her husband pilfered from his master's kitchen. Consumed with jealousy, she began to measure out Kaneez's meals in mean portions, unconcerned that she was going hungry. Finally, Kaneez tried, gently, to fill her husband's ears but he took offence. 'If you say a single word about my mother, there'll be no one worse than I. My mother worked with her nose to the grindstone, trying to bring me up. Everything in this house is hers.'

For all her efforts to show her mother-in-law in a bad light and win her husband round to her way of thinking, Kaneez only succeeded in alienating him. He began avoiding her. There were constant rows. She tormented her mother-in-law who swore back at her, cried and screamed, day in and day out, and wasn't content even after gaining the sympathies of the entire neighbourhood. Spitefully, she doled out such meagre amounts of food to Kaneez, it wasn't enough to line her belly. When Kaneez pushed her way into the kitchen to eat, the hag's invective became ferocious. Her husband, fed up with the loud and constant bickering, hit her and she wreaked her revenge on her mother-in-law. Despite her father's death, she threatened to leave home and her mother-in-law, looking pleased, taunted, 'Where can you go?' And true enough, Kaneez's threat remained a threat.

Then for a few days the fights stopped because she was due to have a baby. After a month's confinement, she arose from her bed with her infant in her arms, but her mother-in-law couldn't bear her to have the power acquired from mothering a son. Nor could she bear the thought of her only son falling under his wife's influence because of it. Kaneez turned tigress. As soon as she was strong enough, she grabbed her mother-in-law by her hair and beat her. That night, her husband and mother-in-law snatched the suckling boy from her breast and threw her out.

She didn't know the town, whose help to seek, where to find refuge. Tangled in her *burqa*, she was walking aimlessly, when the wife of the local *tonga-walla* saw her. She had often visited Kaneez and regaled her, in foul language, with the neighbourhood gossip. Now she took her home and showed her great tenderness but she could not stem her tears. Kaneez beat her breast and wept, lamenting as she pointed to the drops of milk soaking through her shirt. That night when the *tonga-*

walla parked his horse and cart, his bizarre friends came uninhibitedly into the house, whispering and mumbling. Then they locked the doors and began to gamble and smoke pot. The wife sat with them on the floor smoking a reefer, then forced Kaneez to have a whole one, too.

This was her first experience of hashish. It blew her senseless and she fell on the bed, calling out to her baby, her jewel, all night. A few days later, when her tears had not yet abated, the *tonga-walla*'s wife told her that a friend of her husband's had fallen in love with her. Crying would not do. If she wanted to enjoy herself, she should run away with him. He was promising her a life of luxury. Kaneez refused, insisting she wanted a reunion with her husband and mother-in-law. She would endure anything if they took her back. She'd go hungry but wouldn't say a word. If they forbade her to hold her baby, she wouldn't stretch out her arms; if she was told not to look at him, she'd blind herself. She just wanted to be near him. In the end, the *tonga-walla* went to see her husband to get an agreement but he returned with the divorce papers. Like a madwoman, Kaneez tore her hair, pummelled her flesh, shrieked and cried. Her new lover consoled her with all his heart. The *tonga-walla* tenderly reassured and sustained her with a flood of invective against her oppressors but nothing made sense to her. She called to her baby all night, spoke to him, shrieked incessantly and smoked hashish.

Two weeks went by and eventually the *tonga-walla*'s wife said she could support her no longer. Kaneez had a perfect suitor and she should set up home with him. So, at last, she agreed to leave on condition that she could see her jewel just one last time.

But she discovered that her husband and his mother had moved to another town. After the news she neither cried nor lamented, just fell silent as if she'd turned to stone. The very next day her lover took her to a bleak, little-known alley of the town where she soon discovered that he made a living from theft. She didn't object. Whatever he brought home from the sleight of his hand, he cast into her lap. And though he laid himself out with adoration, she couldn't find a civil word to say to him. She swore at him at every turn, smoked heaps of hashish and languished in bed. But thieves and scoundrels just want a woman and the wretch had found a woman after a long time. He wouldn't say an angry word to her. And many days passed that way.

Confined to bed, she had herself examined by all the local mid-wives and found out quite quickly that she was infertile because her mother-in-law had skimped on a proper midwife. After this revelation she became even stranger than before. She lay in bed, beat her breast, swore, smoked and ate so excessively that she messed up her system.

A year later, she insisted that she would help her man by going to work for a rich woman. He was pleased with the idea and very soon taught her the simpler tricks of the trade. As a precaution, he also taught her to break locks and a few days later, she relinquished her *burqa* and began staking out houses to make his job easier. Now the two were in clover. Instead of crying and lamenting, she laughingly devoured litres of milk and stopped being so nasty to her lover. Then, one day, who knows what got into her – instead of stealing her mistress's possessions, she abducted her suckling infant. But she was caught soon enough, smothering the child with kisses. She and her partner were jailed for seven months each, with hard labour. They met after their release and returned to work in the obscure streets. But her partner warned her that if she did something so foolish again, she would die for nothing. A proper 'Godfather' doesn't get caught by the police. And when she asked him the meaning of Godfather, she learned that that was the name they used for crime lords in Bombay and that he had lived for quite a while with such crime lords.

Two or three days later, she demanded he call her 'Godfather' in future. If he called her Kaneez again, she would smash in both their skulls. Her lover tried to convince her that the title was inappropriate for women but she repudiated her womanhood. After she assumed the name of Godfather, she started to stake out houses again and once, without consultation, burgled clumsily. She was imprisoned for a month and her lover was forced to suffer a six-month sentence. This time when they met after their release, Godfather's behaviour was more bizarre than ever before. So much so, that even her lover couldn't understand her. She would roam the streets in broad daylight wielding her stick. Her partner and his criminal friends warned her she would get everyone in trouble if she carried on like this but she didn't care. She wandered around, got smashed on pot and crashed out in bed. Finally, fed up with her ignoring all his pleas and warnings, her partner abandoned her. She lay hungry and thirsty for ages, watching the sky. That night she broke into a house with a big bang and ended up in jail for six months.

When she was released she sat hungry and thirsty in the lane where she had lived with her lover. As night fell, she arose, weary, and went to the house of an acquaintance who had given up crime. She begged some food from him and then, stealing the stick that stood in his porch, she left.

Night's darkness was growing more hideous but she walked along that tarmacked road, tapping her stick, thinking who knows what and then very soon afterwards she was standing, staring at the sentry, as if to say, 'Brother, let me walk my fill today, I'm in despair. Life feels tragic tonight. Let me walk . . .'

She spent a night and a day of silence in prison. The next day when she began peeping, like a cat, through the iron railing, there was not a shadow of grief on her face. When the warden passed her cell, she called out, 'Oi! Say something, will you? You walk around like a machine.' The warden walked past glaring and Godfather swore like a man and guffawed.

Locked up in solitary, she was badly in need of hashish. On her previous spells in prison there had been no shortage of it. The lack of it unbalanced her. Her body ached so much, she fell ill. The prison doctor examined her but prescribed such bitter medicine that she smashed the bottle and leapt around the cell, frightening her.

One day Godfather tried to suck up to the volunteer prisoner who was distributing the food.

'Can I get some dope somewhere, sweetie?'

'No!' the volunteer said, but took pity on her and gave her two *bidis*.

'If you get me some, I'll give you two rupees.' Godfather tried bribing her with money she had managed to conceal in spite of all the searches.

'No. My God, if an officer found out, I'd lose my pardon. I've got to get out fast. I have small children.' The woman's eyes filled with tears. After that Godfather never mentioned dope to her again. Instead, she began pestering the other prison workers, swearing when they refused.

Today, a month later, Godfather had been to court to hear her sentence. She listened in silence to the proceedings but when she heard her life sentence pronounced, she clashed her handcuffs and shouted, 'I don't want fourteen years in prison. If I'm alive after that will the judge give me a home?' She swore loudly as the female wardens dragged her away.

'Hey, you bastard! You dog! Why are you giving me just fourteen years?' The female guards thrust her into the car and she swore all the way to the prison. Half the day had gone by the time they arrived. She was given a prison uniform and a blanket and left in barrack no. 2. When she went in, all the prisoners were out on exercise. Wrapped in their black blankets and mattresses, she saw row upon row of aluminium cups. She swore under her breath and her face, ravaged from lack of a fix, looked vile. For a while, she paced up and down and when the prisoners returned and began to agitate in anticipation of their meal, she almost hissed with anger: 'Hey – bastards! Shut up. Or I'll kill someone else and get another fourteen years.'

'Who do you think you are, you bitch?' a woman responded immediately. Godfather rolled up her sleeves and the other women had to pull them apart. Godfather fought with several other women through the night, and the wardens watched her as she tossed and turned restlessly in bed.

When they were served cold chick-peas for breakfast, she stood at the front of the queue, bright and alert. 'Give me some more! This lot won't even fill a corner of my belly.' The volunteer took pity on her strapping frame and ladled out some more.

'Me too, sister,' the woman behind Godfather cooed.

'If you bitches want luxury, stay at home in peace.' The woman picked up her bucket. 'Swear at any one again,' threatened Godfather, 'and I'll smash your head.' She lunged for the bucket and though she couldn't get any food, she was lashed six times as an example to the other women. Then they were all sent out to work. The thrashing did not have the desired effect. The women who had fought her all of last night were making up to her now.

'Sister, what have you been convicted for?' a woman asked as she sat mending a prisoner's clothes.

'Sister,' Godfather minced, mimicking the woman. 'Don't dare call me "sister". My name is Godfather, *Godfather*. I curse the female species! Do you know who a Godfather is? A crime-lord. I'm not a woman, I'm a criminal. I'm here for killing someone.'

Godfather announced it loudly. The other women looked at her in consternation.

'Is there any dope around, my love?' Godfather whispered, sidling up to a woman who had smoked *bidis* incessantly, through the night.

'Shabratan may have some,' the woman said, pointing to the prisoner because of whom Godfather had fielded the six blows earlier.

'Any *charas*?' Godfather was severely troubled for lack of it. The *bidi* she had begged tasted of straw.

'Any money?' Shabratan whispered back, efficiently weaving her basket.

'Yes.' Godfather produced a rupee note from her pinafore and held it out and Shabratan pulled out a reefer from the waist of her *shalwar* and handed it over.

'A rupee for a cigarette?'

'Yes, sir,' Shabratan replied dismissively. Godfather lost her temper.

'OK, so take another rupee.' Godfather grabbed her hair and pulled her close. Chaos broke out among the women. Godfather grabbed back her rupee before anyone could find out the cause of the trouble. But it was with some difficulty that the others pulled them apart.

The women in Godfather's barrack soon acquired grievances against her. 'She's always picking fights.' Several times she was reported to the assistant superintendent with a request for her transfer. But who listened to the women's complaints? Their fights were a daily affair. Godfather was just another trouble-maker. Her workload was increased a bit. But what difference would that have made to her? She dealt with the hardest job in a pinch. Finally, to get rid of her, the women of the barrack stopped communicating with her. But even that made no difference. She jibed and tormented and forced Shabratan to supply her with free pot and though she swore she had no more, Godfather continued to freeload, threatening to report her to the superintendent. Shabratan's friend, for whom she was enduring this year in prison, managed to get piles of dope to her by who knows what means and she got the other women addicted to it and sold it at inflated prices. But this freeloading Godfather, curse her, was a particular blight on Shabratan. Other women received visitors who secretly passed money to them and Shabratan would question her haplessly: 'Godfather, don't you have anyone? No lover or friend?'

'I've got you, haven't I? You'll keep me supplied, won't you?' Godfather would extend a hand towards her *shalwar* and Shabratan would stand up with a start.

Apart from the free dope, Godfather forcefully took a share of the food the women were brought during visits. She fought them for it and if she didn't get it through force, she stole it at night. Then she shared it with women who, like her, didn't have visitors.

When the women saw their food had gone, they beat their breasts and cried and fought with Godfather but she didn't care a jot. Several times, she was lashed and had her labour increased but for all her troublemaking and stealing of food, when the prison doctor visited, she lay down, groaning: 'I'm so weak, Doctor, I can't even manage to swallow a crust of bread. Please prescribe some milk for me.'

Immediately, the others contradicted her: 'Doctor, she not only gobbles every crust of her own food, she steals everyone else's.'

The doctor grinned and left without examining Godfather.

Sometimes the frailer women were given milk and Godfather swore foully at the women who had prevented her getting any. Finally, she did get herself a week's quota. That day she gloated, triumphant: 'Go on, complain a bit more about me. I'll just drink my milk.' She laughed loudly, tormenting them.

It was customary for Godfather to fight, grab someone's hair, then beat someone else but she had some quiet days – so very quiet she failed to respond even to abuse. Sometimes she hid her face and cried secretly, then dried her tears, menaced Shabratan and smoked piles of pot.

The days passed – the women in Godfather's barrack came and went, apart from Shabratan. Old and recent, they all knew Godfather. She still fought them for their food and drink but she protected them from the maltreatment of the wardens. Once she even beat up the superintendent for condemning a woman to four days in solitary, for insolence. She beat her in the presence of all the other women. Godfather received ten lashes for that and her privileges were revoked. Now the women confided their woes to her and at night when they sobbed, missing their homes, Godfather would comfort them with tenderly spoken swearwords, dry their tears, share their sadness and fall silent.

This evening a very young, slim woman was brought into Godfather's barrack, carrying an infant, barely two months old. The moment she arrived, the mother sat down on the ground, put the baby to her breast and began weeping. The prisoners gathered round her and asked why she was here. What was her crime? The mother didn't answer, crying more and more intensely. The women offered her water and calmed her – only Godfather sat at a distance, glowering. When the mother, exhausted from crying, grew silent, Godfather edged over to her: 'Wonderful, my little bridie, commit a crime, then cry. If you were so frail-hearted, you should have sat at home prim and proper.'

'What's my crime?' The mother flared up, then resumed crying. 'I've been framed.'

'Framed how?' Godfather asked with a bit of sympathy.

'My husband married again within a year of our wedding,' the mother began telling her story. 'I wept and cried but then I contained myself so that I would not deprive my unborn baby of his father. I lived like a servant in my own home. That wasn't enough for my husband. He would say, "I want you, personally, to make up the bed for me and my new wife." I placed a stone on my heart and did it.' She sighed and dabbed her tears.

'Even after that I was a thorn in his new wife's side. One day she lay down and started to scream that she had been poisoned. The whole neighbourhood gathered round. When the doctor examined her it turned out that she had taken too much opium. When the police arrived she told them I had poisoned her. The house was searched, so was I, and some opium was discovered tied in my *dupatta*. I don't know when she put it there. The police took me to the station and from there to prison. I've been in another barrack since then. My father was winning the case, then goodness knows how he lost, and I've received a six-month sentence, suspended for three months because of the baby. I'm a good woman – how will I show my face when I leave here? My father's honour has been sullied.' She started sobbing again.

'Hunh, but you ass, why did you live like a slave in your own husband's home? You should have got out the same day and got another lover and you wouldn't be here today,' Godfather said passionately. Then she tugged the sleeping baby's leg and cleared her throat. 'You've dragged along this pup. You should have hurled him in his father's face and said, "You look after him." Here, give him to me for a bit.' Godfather took the baby tenderly in her arms.

'And here, you smoke this,' she offered a half-smoked reefer to his mother.

'I don't smoke. And look here, don't swear at my child again. I'm here because of him or I would have jumped from the roof of my home and killed myself.'

'"My baby, my baby". Who do you think you are, you mother you?

Take him back.' Godfather lifted the child as if he was a mouse and thrust him at his mother. Then she cursed him, secretly, for hours.

That night Godfather tossed and turned, looking at the child and burbling who knows what, when usually she slept deeply, snoring, oblivious to the bites of the fleas in her blanket.

Godfather suddenly reverted to the state she had been in when she first came to prison, fighting, causing trouble, being foul-mouthed. She was particularly hostile to the woman with the baby. She would snatch the baby from her then shove him back unceremoniously.

'"My baby". Who do you think you are, just because you have a baby?', Godfather would growl and the woman looked at her, perplexed, and hugged the child close, crying so broken-heartedly that all the women cursed Godfather. If the baby woke in the night, crying, Godfather paced the floor: 'Shut the little whelp up. You've dumped him on us to blight our sleep.'

'Look, Godfather, you're picking a fight for no reason. Which child doesn't cry?', some woman tried reasoning with her.

'Then let them cry but why destroy my sleep? Let our little bride suppress the baby's voice.'

'And wouldn't I rather suppress your voice,' the mother retorted, trembling with fury, then sobbing helplessly. 'Hai! Hai! My mother.'

Godfather fell silent but while the other women slept at night, she tossed and turned. One day the baby developed a slight fever. His mother was beside herself with tears. Tenderly, Godfather begged to be allowed to hold the baby. But when the doctor came, she immediately ordered Godfather to hand the baby back, insisting she would hear his symptoms from his mother. Godfather obliged but her blood began to boil. The mother wept as she spoke: 'Doctor, my baby's terribly ill. He was unconscious all night – he didn't open his eyes, my jewel, his forehead was blazing like a fire.'

'He's not had a fever or anything, Doctor,' Godfather butted in, resentfully. 'He howled all night and she claims he was unconscious.' The doctor motioned Godfather to silence, examined the child, then wrote a prescription and had it administered in her presence.

Today the woman's father was visiting and he brought some clothes and little toys for the baby. The woman looked pleased.

'My father says he's organized my divorce and I'll be marrying his brother's son,' she said happily. 'My cousin has always been in love with me. He wouldn't marry after losing me. And everything else apart, he'll take my baby to his heart.'

'Oh, so you have a lover,' Godfather interrupted. 'This love thing is short-lived, you know. Don't fantasize, it won't last.'

'Don't let it last – at least I have a son. He'll sustain me for the rest of my life. What's it to you?' The woman was put out and sulked silently.

Tomorrow the mother and baby will be released. Today, Godfather tried forcefully to hold the baby but the woman wouldn't let her touch him once. Nor did she respond to her baiting. She was so happy, she could hardly sleep at night. She sang lullabies and kissed her baby and Godfather looked wretched.

'Shut up and go to sleep, you accursed creature,' Godfather screamed again and again but the woman ignored her and didn't sleep until past midnight.

When she was deeply asleep and silence filled the barrack, Godfather sat up in her bed. She looked around stealthily. A light bulb shone down on her from a farm far above. 'Barrack no. 1, Barrack no. 2. Everything's fine – Everything is fine.' Outside the voices of the wardens called to each other. Godfather crawled softly to the bed of the mother and baby.

At dawn, the blanket was removed from Godfather's mattress. There was an uproar. The prison officers gathered round and the baby's mother beat her breast, screaming, smashing her face with stones, falling on the floor from an upright position. Godfather's shirt was tied tightly around her neck and the baby, lying on her breast, held her milkless teat in his mouth. Their eyes protruded from their orbs and their bodies were cold and stiff.

Translated by Shahrukh Husain

Hijab Imtiaz Ali

And He Had an Accident

Laid on a stretcher, he was brought to the operating theatre. Today he had been looking around, standing in the balcony of the upper storey of his house. The morning was brilliant and extremely beautiful, when all of a sudden he fell several feet to the ground. Apparently no one had pushed him, neither had the floor of the balcony been so weak that it had given way under his load. Then how had he fallen down? By the way, what was so strange about it? It was an accident like the ones that keep on happening every day. Even he himself was not conscious enough to think over this matter. Nor was he the nit-picking sort. It's obvious that it was a slip of the foot that made him lose his balance and fall from such a great height. As far as words were concerned, this explanation seemed good enough: he had fallen due to loss of balance, and accidents do happen that way.

When he was brought to the operating theatre, although his body was unfeeling and motionless like a corpse, his mind bore the vast agitation of the ocean. The same ebb and flow, the same stormy billows – the human brain is never devoid of anxiety and strife.

He was totally unaware of his surroundings. He could see neither the white caps of the nurses nor the masked faces of the doctors. His eyes were sightless to the glare of the bright lights of the operating theatre and his ears deaf to the sound of scissors and scalpels. It was so because when we behold even an ant in our past, we are unconscious of a mountain in the present. He had no knowledge of why he was brought there, yet the ears of his memory and his mind's eye could see far in the distance.

'Munoo! Munoo!' The voice fell in his ears. He wondered whose name it was, still reverberating in the deep valleys of the past. And suddenly he remembered that Munoo was a puppy that he had borrowed from his friend and lovingly looked after. Munoo was so tiny that it could not even suck milk and so the whole night long it would moan in its pain-filled voice which disgusted the neighbours. And quite apart from the neighbours, his own mother had an unreasonable hatred for the puppy!

So many times his mother had scolded him angrily, 'Get rid of this puppy or I'll poison it! The wretch keeps on screaming the whole night through!'

But today, after so many years, why was he reminded of Munoo? He was now thirty years old and Munoo was a forgotten silliness of his childhood!

Then it so happened that Munoo was not poisoned but nature itself turned against it. While romping on the road, it was run over by a bicycle. After this accident, Munoo became the apple of his mother's eye. Ointment was bought for Munoo's wounds, from the market. The puppy was treated and bandaged. A new bed was made and its untimely wailing was tolerated with fortitude. Poor puppy! It was injured. He realized that this dangerous accident had made the puppy pitiable in the eyes of his mother.

Gradually the sound of Munoo's wailing faded and another incident of recent years rose on the curtain of his mind. That day on Friday, he got leave from the office a little early. On the way home, he decided to go boating with his wife Feroza and take some refreshments along as well. En route was the house of a good friend. He went there and invited him to join them too. Momentarily he thought that the friend he had invited was disliked by his wife. She might be displeased, but then, he thought that he would persuade her. After all, Ahmad was not as bad as she thought. No denying that he was a liar but who doesn't lie? He bought chicken sandwiches and cheese fingers from a restaurant and hurried home.

Carrying bags of snacks, he wanted to shout with joy like a child while hugging Feroza, and tell her that he had got an extra holiday. On reaching home he cried out, 'Feroza! Feroza! Look what I've brought! We were let off from the office early today!'

His wife, leaving her chores, came into the room.

'Whatever have you brought?'

'Chicken sandwiches and cheese fingers! We're going boating!' he said laughingly.

'A holiday from the office makes you as excited as a kid escaping from school,' she teased him.

A little offended, he said, 'If you went to the office every day, you'd understand that its rules and regulations mean the same to us as school and captivity mean to a child. OK, put all these things in a tiffin basket and fill up a thermos flask with tea. We have to rush as I've told Ahmad to arrange for a boat. He'll be waiting for us on the beach.'

'Why do we need Ahmad to accompany us?' she said, somewhat displeased. 'The boat could've been arranged easily once we'd reached the seaside. I don't like Ahmad's loud ways.'

'You're being unreasonable. He's all right. Why are you so put off by him?' he said.

'Well, because he's a tittle-tattle! He carries a tale from one person and relates it to another. Isn't this enough? I hate such dangerous people!'

He laughed. 'Such people are the life and soul of the party. Just forgive him this time and don't show your displeasure so obviously. He noticed it last time too.'

'Still he agreed to come today? Who would like such shamelessness?' Feroza said scornfully.

'OK! OK! Put up with him just for today. I'll never invite him again. He'll be waiting for us on the shore right now.'

And they reached the seaside.

By pure coincidence, this small party had been boating for not even half an hour when a dark cloud rose, a strong gale blew and the gusts of wind hit so hard that they lost control of the craft and it overturned.

After an hour, he and his wife reached the shore safely but Ahmad was not to be found. Everybody thought he had been drowned. Somebody said that he had been eaten by the fish. Someone else said that he must have fainted from loss of breath and been carried away by the waves.

He felt that this tragic accident had had a great impact on Feroza. She said in a sad, tearful voice, 'Alas! Who knew that Ahmad would be separated from us like this?'

'I thought you'd be happy!' he commented sarcastically.

'I wasn't his enemy.'

But the next day, the fishermen found an unconscious Ahmad.

Before bringing him to his house to be looked after, he first spoke to his wife. 'If you don't disagree, may I bring Ahmad here? He can go back to his own home after he feels better.'

Feroza answered emotionally, 'Do bring him here. This accident in the water has washed away my hatred.'

And Ahmad was brought to his house.

He noticed that this accident had changed his wife's attitude completely. Earlier, she couldn't even tolerate Ahmad's presence but now the same Feroza felt pleasure in looking after all his needs.

He thought that this accident had made Ahmad someone deserving of pity in the eyes of Feroza.

He felt a certain similarity between his mother and his wife. Munoo's incident and now this event! Both women were similar in this respect, but poles apart in others. Who would tolerate a woman who did not resemble his mother in some ways? If Feroza had been a totally different woman from his mother, so different – like day is from night – she could have been acceptable. But his perplexity was that although seemingly alike they were still dissimilar. Alas! This had caused conflict. The heart's perturbation had increased.

A few days before today's accident, he had started feeling a little aggrieved with his wife. He loved her deeply but at the same time his heart was full of complaints against her. He could never see his grievances in a practical way; how could he? He was himself unaware of the reason for these grievances. Then how could he quarrel with his wife or complain about her?

He remembered. One night he and his wife had argued over some small matter. When he got up in the morning he felt ill. He was sure that his wife would be anxious because of his pain and maybe even massage his head. But it didn't happen like that. Feroza gave him a frowning look and said, 'It's time for the office. Get up, have your breakfast and leave.' And he didn't know how his fever vanished and his headache disappeared.

In minutes he was ready and gone. But sorrow and depression made him slack and idle. In the afternoon a friend took him along to his house. He played cards with him all evening and his dejection apparently dissipated. But when he was climbing the steps to his own house, his anger resurfaced unconsciously and a sea of despair appeared in his eyes. In low spirits, he passed by his wife and went to his room.

'What's wrong with you, darling? Come to me!' His wife's loving words echoed in his waiting ears. Forgetting everything, he was about to run to his wife when he realized that this was not her voice but the sound of the radio in the upper storey. A play was being broadcast – perhaps his ears had heard what they were yearning for. Whatever it was, it wasn't his wife speaking. He stood still and depression swept over him.

Next day, he was standing on the balcony of his upper storey, looking around. The morning was brilliant and extremely beautiful when suddenly – all at once, no one knows how – he fell several feet to the ground. And his wife left all her numerous tasks to sit by his bedside – yes! By his bedside!

And that is how accidents happen!

Translated by Atiya Shah

Mumtaz Shirin

The Awakening

'*Apa*, Gulnar *Apa*! Look, Miss Fen . . .' Javaid was tugging at my sari with his tiny hands.

'*Arrey*, get off! *Apa*, *Apa*, all the time. Look, how you're ruining my fresh white sari with these grubby, filthy hands! Were you playing with mud, you ill-mannered wretch?' I angrily slapped his hand away. He screwed up his face. 'No, *Apa*. Miss Fence is on our road . . .', he sobbed. 'Please call her . . . Miss Fence is so nice. She gave me cake and cocoa . . . nice cocoa. Please call her, *Apa*. Sweet *Apa*.'

'*Arrey*!' I was startled. 'Miss Fence, here?' I glanced at the window, yes it really was Miss Fence in the distance, walking this way, talking to some woman. 'So, should I call her?' I thought. I took a quick look round the room. Books scattered everywhere, and the furniture! One chair lay in the corner with its face to the wall and one plumb in the middle of the room, as if preening itself on its unpolished surface. And the sofa! Hunh! The filthy stuffing spilt out of a gaping hole. Tablecloth? Javaid had made generous use of ink in drawing patterns on it! My God, is anything in order? *Uf*! What ill-mannered fool has scattered the papers on the floor? Does anyone else have such mischievous children? And this inch-thick layer of dust . . .! Is Kariman dead? The unfortunate wretch can't even be bothered to sweep the rooms early in the morning.

'Kariman, O Kariman! Bring the duster. Have you gathered this dust to sell?'

'Coming, *Bibi*! Just coming. Let me take the bread off the griddle, it'll burn.'

To hell with her and her bread. She's such a miserable one, always stuck in the oven . . . Why was I so agitated, I asked myself, beginning to feel ashamed of my behaviour. The poor woman was alone and all the housework was on her head. We weren't so well off that we could afford ten servants. Even one was a blessing.

I quickly changed the tablecloth and dragging the chairs to their place began gathering the papers scattered all over the floor. While gathering the papers I glanced out of the window. Miss Fence had stopped! How close she was! 'Zakia! Zubeida!' I gave a full-throated shout. No answer! I went to the door, looked out and felt a murderous rage on seeing both present in the courtyard. Zakia was standing holding Javaid while Zubeida had climbed onto the gate and was craning her neck to catch a glimpse of Miss Fence.

'Zakia, have you any intention of helping? Aren't you ashamed of yourself standing out there like this?'

'Why are you getting angry, *Apa*! It's not as if I'm always at the gate. Just today . . . like that . . .' She laughed as she caught sight of my peeved expression.

'Aha! *Apa*, today your mercury is soaring at a hundred degrees! See if I don't say something to bring down my *Apa's* temperature. Shall I tell you something really interesting?' She pulled a face and clapped, 'Shall I, *Apa*? . . . Oho . . . Miss Fence is passing this way!'

'I know all that. Come here and help me clean up the room. You only know how to chatter.' I was offhand with her.

'So, *Apa*, are you going to call Miss Fence?' she asked, jumping up and down with joy. Zubeida was also dancing. How is it that these children are still so fond of Miss Fence?

I snapped at Zakia, who was staring at the door again. The papers were still scattered all over the room.

'Hunh! I'm not going to call her, considering the state of the house.' I irritably threw the papers I had gathered on the floor.

'What are you saying, *Apa*?' Zakia was looking at me in surprise.

I ignored her and called out to Zubeida: 'Zubeida! Javaid! Go in.'

'Why, *Apa*?' Zubeida asked as she entered.

'Come here. If Miss Fence sees you she'll find out that this is our house and she's bound to want to see me.' I dragged Javaid in as well.

'That'll be wonderful! Why shouldn't she come, *Apa*?'

'Seen the condition of your beautiful home?'

'We'll settle everything. Please let her come, *Apa*,'they both pleaded enthusiastically.

'I've told you I'm not going to call her.'

'Oh, *Apa*. It's been so long since we've had a chance to see Miss Fence. Hasn't it been two or three months since you left college? After so long, purely by chance she's in our city and she's passing by our house and you, you're not going to call her in? *Apa,* you're being . . .' Zakia stopped in the midst of her harangue and laughed, giving me a mischievous look. 'Right! Now I know . . . ever since Parvaiz *bhaiyya . . .*'

'*Arri*, quiet! You've started making such fancy speeches.' I pinched her hard.

'You're a pretender, *Apa*. See how coy you got at the mention of Parvaiz's name.'

I stood there shy, blushing, shrinking inside, lost, as if the name had cast a spell on me. What a beautiful name! What a wonderful name! Parvaiz.

I awoke from my reverie to find the portals of the doors wide open, the curtain flapping in the wind and Miss Fence standing bang opposite our house, fixing me with her eyes. As I caught her gaze, she smiled and began moving towards it.

'Oh! God! What is to be done now?' I shook Zakia. 'You see to everything. Look, she's coming here.'

I quickly ran from there, only stopping to breathe once I was in my room. A little later when I peeped out, I saw Miss Fence sitting in the room adjacent to the verandah and Zakia standing next to her carrying an attractive dish of bananas and oranges.

'Call Gulnar,' Miss Fence was saying. Suddenly she saw me

peeping and smiled and called out, 'Gulnar!' I retreated shyly behind the door . . . What must she have made of my coy behaviour? Just that I still had the same feelings for her. Hunh! How was she to know that I now . . . but she must be harbouring the same wrong impression . . .

I had always been shy in front of her, running away when she appeared. When she looked at me I would hide my face in both hands although I wanted her to keep looking. What a strange girl I was some years back! Gradually I had opened up with her. Even then, when we ran into each other unexpectedly you should have seen my confusion! What days those were! It was usual for me to wait hours for her in the verandah after the bell had rung. The week when we had no classes with her was the most miserable week of all. Yes, I doted on her. I loved her to distraction. How the girls would tease me: 'Gulnar, we don't know why you dote on Miss Fence, she's no beauty. In fact, it wouldn't be far wrong to call her ugly.' Those witches, if only I could have scratched their faces! How would they know how beautiful she looked to me? I was annoyed with Zarina, although she was my dearest friend. I remember wearing a black sari that day and had borrowed a black *bindiya* from Purva to put on. Zarina and I were strolling in the hostel compound when Indira had appeared from somewhere . . . 'Aha! You're looking devilishly beautiful today, Gulnar.'

'Like Miss Fence?' I had blurted out inadvertently.

'Hunh, Miss Fence!' Zarina had said sarcastically. 'Miss Fence! She'd have to die and be reborn thrice over to acquire your beauty!'

I had been so angry with her.

'Annoyed with me, Gul? All right, she's five times more beautiful than you! Happy now?' She had gone into peals of laughter and Indira had smiled as well. I felt like killing Zarina. After all, who was she to insult Miss Fence? If a single word was said against her, I was prepared to fight with the entire college. I was not alone. Many girls would have supported me as so many were in love with her. Zarina was different, she would place no obstacles in my path but would be happy to see Miss Fence indulge me. What a selfless girl she was!

In contrast, there was that Lakshmi! She was awfully, terribly jealous of me. She made every effort to turn Miss Fence's attention away, from me to her. All those beautiful saris she'd brought and her put-on manner and specially designed pearl jewellery! She'd even had her hair curled with an electrical appliance! Hunh! What was the point of all the effort since she was not beautiful anyway? Miss Fence would only have to look at me for her to be consumed with jealousy. Despite reading hundreds of books on Miss Fence's special subject, could she write better than me? Had she ever scored more marks than me? When nothing worked her envy would take over, and she would always be on the look-out for an opportunity to make a hurtful remark. How she would fret when she heard people call me beautiful! Her response would be: 'Hunh! Can anyone be called beautiful who doesn't have a pink and white complexion? Height and a slim body are the prerequisites of beauty.' Not that she was fair, but she was tall and slender, although there was no beauty in her thin body. She looked as if a long piece of wood had been whittled bare. There were no pleasing contours to her shape. No suppleness and no style. A flat, lifeless piece of wood! I really wanted to shut her up. 'Hunh! For beauty, charming features are far more important than a fair complexion and a full, rounded body is as beautiful as a delicate one, in fact it is far more attractive.' But I would smile and maintain my silence. I didn't want her to feel that she had succeeded in needling me.

Sometimes she would show me a fair-complexioned girl and say, 'Look, Gulnar, how beautiful that girl is.' And the girl she was pointing out would be so ugly, so repulsive-looking that I would burst out laughing. Squashed nose, spreading nostrils, very thick lips, clumsy body but yes, she would have a fair colouring! I would say 'Lakshmi, I salute your sense of beauty!' When this would not work she'd descend straight to the personal level, jeering and calling me 'black' although my complexion is clearly wheatish . . .

And then there was Zeenat, who just would not leave Miss Fence alone. How artlessly she would complain, 'Gulnar! Miss Fence likes you the best.' And what about that enormously fat girl . . . more of a woman than a girl! She lived and breathed for Miss Fence, and what peculiar ways she had of demonstrating her love, making even Miss Fence laugh out aloud! And Nalini . . .

'Gulnar Bibi!'

'What is it, Kariman?'

'*Begum* has asked me to make French toast and *samosas*. You know that some Miss *Sahiba* has come visiting. I have so much work, daughter, can you cut these pieces of bread? My sweet child, I'll always serve you faithfully.'

I opened the door and peeped cautiously to see if Miss Fence was looking this way. *Ammi* was sitting near her and they were busy talking. I tiptoed quickly into the kitchen and, cleaning the knife throughly, sat down to slice the bread. Kariman put the cooked mince on the stove, added some salt, pepper and onions and began to brown it. So French toast is being made, is it? It was such a favourite of Miss Fence's! How many times had I made it with my own hands and sent it to her in the days she had been a professor in a local college and how I had wept when she had been transferred! She had talked to me and tried to console me but I had not been able to stop my tears. After weeping my fill, I had persuaded *Abba* to send me to the same place where Miss Fence was working and had met up with her. Two years passed in a flash. I had to appear for the final college exam and then be parted from Miss Fence for ever, I couldn't bear the thought of that. How I wished that the college had offered an M.A. course so I could have spent another two years with her! I had even toyed with the idea of failing that year. For a girl who had always come top in her class, to fail was particularly shameful but that never bothered me. The professors had such high hopes of me. I would win many medals and prizes at the convocation. To come first among the girls was usual for me and there would be special medals for that, but I would also head the state list in sociology and English. The boys would be thunderstruck and the name of the college would be writ in letters of gold . . . but now I didn't care if I dashed their hopes.

The final day of the examination arrived and I went to meet Miss Fence for the last time. When I returned to the hostel after saying goodbye, I went straight to my room, threw myself on the bed and, hiding my face in the pillows, wept bitterly. The flood of tears made my eyes red and the bedcover damp. Zarina, when she came, embraced me and began consoling me. The more she comforted me the more bitterly I wept. That night Zarina sat with me for a long time, explaining things to me so that my stinging eyes began to close under the pressure of sleep. What a loving person Zarina had been!

'Finished cutting the pieces, daughter? Hand them over so I can fry them in *ghee*, and, dear child, just fill the pancakes with mince and make the *samosas*. *Begum* has asked for them quickly. What can I do, daughter! You can see how old I've grown. Can't do that much with my hands or would I have asked you to work? Heaven forgive me! May this old mouth become infested with worms for ever uttering such words! Such delicate hands are fit only for holding a pen, how can I, a mere maidservant, desire to see them perform menial tasks? May God blind me before I wish that for you!' Old Kariman started flattering me. I filled the pancakes with mince and started making the *samosas* without replying.

How Miss Fence had loved me, calling me to her home many times and insisting that I accompany her on her walks. How she had begged that day, 'Just come once, Gulnar! I'll take you for a drive in my car. I'll take you to such and such a garden.' My hurt pride had made me spurn her offers. And then how generously she would mark me! Eighty or eighty-five per cent! Seeing this, the girls would be very envious. They would say, 'Well of course, you're her favourite, aren't you? How could we get such marks?'

When she spoke my name, she would savour it in her mouth like a delicious sweetmeat, and when she smiled at me, how loving that smile was. I would instantly want to call her 'Angelina' instead of Miss Fence, but I had never dared to do that. Though I hesitated to open my mouth before her, I would write whatever came to my mind in my letters. I wrote, 'Queen of my heart', 'My darling', 'Queen of beauty',

'Heavenly Angelina'. Strange romantic letters I would write! And she would never be annoyed. And then one day . . .

One day Lalita and I were sitting with her on the back seat of the car. In conversation Lalita had asked, 'Miss Fence, do you know how to ride?' 'No,' she had replied, 'but I've wanted to learn for a long time and that's why I'm getting a riding kit stitched,' and then turning to me, 'A coat and trousers, Gulnar.' She had said it in such a way that I had dissolved in shame. 'I'll look just like a man in it, won't I?' I sat with my face hidden in both my hands. Yes, there was a glimpse of the man in her. Very tall, a broad, strong chest and her looks would make me blush. Even if she were standing in a crowd, talking to other girls, her eyes would be fixed on me . . . and how good she would look in a tangerine sari. The reflection of the sari would cast a golden glow on her face and there would be a faint blush on her cheeks, tinged with blue, and from a distance her pock-marks would not be visible either . . .

I put the plate of *samosas* in front of Kariman, who started to fry them. I was finally free of all the chores! Sitting in front of the stove for so long had made me feel hot, so I washed my hands and face with cold water, wiped them with the sari ends and turned my eyes towards the room where Miss Fence was sitting. The same magical smile that had cast a spell over me. Now I was ready to meet her . . . till my eye casually fell on my sari. It had dirty patches and Javaid's paw marks were clearly visible. How can I go out in this sari? I saw Zubeida come out.

'Zubeida!' I called. She was running along, not paying any attention. 'Zubeida, come here.'

'Hunh, I won't come. I want to go to Miss Fence.'

'My sweet little one. Listen to *Apa*. I'll give my little one a chocolate.'

'What is it, *Apa*?' Her eyes lit up at the prospect of chocolate.

'Sweet little one, fetch me a sari from the cupboard. See how grubby this one is. How can I wear this and go out to Miss Fence? Here, take the keys to the cupboard.'

'Alright, *Apa*. Go quickly, Miss Fence keeps asking for you.'

She still cared for me. Perhaps. Two months ago I had sent her a letter through another girl, who had reported her joy at receiving it. Had she not been delighted the day I had arrived, without prior warning, at the college where she then worked? I could see her from my hiding place but she couldn't see me and I had sent a girl to inform her that I was seeking admission to that college. In a highly emotional state she had repeated my name several times. 'Gulnar! Gulnar! Gulnar! Is that true?' The girl had assured her it was. 'Where is she? Tell me.' The girl began telling her where I was but without paying any attention to her she had set out to find me. 'Gulnar! Where are you?' I had enjoyed witnessing her impatience.

'Finally everything is prepared. Let me rest this old body for a while . . .'

Old wretch. Always muttering to herself. I was irritated.

'God bless you, Gulnar Bibi. What a help you have been to this old woman.' Kariman spread a piece of jute right there in the kitchen and lay down. 'Oh, there you are, daughter. My Bibi will have a long life. I was just thinking of you, my child! You are in my prayers all the time. I'm not lying. I've worked in many places but no, sir, I've never seen such a girl. In other homes even young lads would tell me off but my Bibi has never said a harsh word to me. Now my days of work are over, which is why I had even left your home. I tell you truthfully, daughter, I only came at the news of your wedding. I've always cherished the desire to see you as a bride with my own eyes. God bless you with a wonderful groom.'

Could there be a groom more wonderful than Parvaiz? A gentle smile appeared on my lips. I hastily turned my face in case Kariman noticed.

Then, all at once, my mind was emptied of all thoughts except: Parvaiz! Parvaiz! . . . and I drifted into this bright, beautiful world. Exceedingly beautiful. Far more than college and the world of Miss Fence.

There was a time when I had wondered whether, if I were to get married, I would be able to love my husband at all. Once Zarina, who knew about palmistry, had looked at my hand and said, 'Your husband will love you enormously.' And I had felt such pity for my would-be husband, thinking that I would not be able to respond to his love. And now? Now see how madly I care for my Parvaiz!

'*Apa*, here's the sari.' I took the sari from Zubeida, put it on the table and began combing my hair.

How was I able to forget Miss Fence? She had cared for me a great deal. Cares a great deal. Had she ever expressed it verbally? When I was with her she was deathly afraid. 'Gulnar, what must the girls be saying? Gulnar, if the principal sees us, what then?'

If the girls see us, let them. Had we committed a crime to be so fearful? Oh, the faint-heartedness! And when she brought the corrected copies to class she would be brimming with fulsome praise for my ideas and point of view but would never tell the girls that they were mine. Returning the answer sheets she would never even take my name, but she would give me the highest marks . . . Hunh, was this any way to behave? I would come first in every paper, but no teacher would give me such high marks as Miss Fence, who would give up to eighty or eighty-five per cent. So what if she gave me high marks? I would have been so happy if she had praised me in class in front of all the girls and said, 'See how many marks Gulnar has got.' Instead of, 'Such and such a roll number has got so many marks, such and such a roll number has done this, done that, done the other, such and such a roll number, such and such a roll number . . .' I had been reduced to 'such and such a roll number'.

Even Miss Jones with her M.A. from Oxford would spend half an hour at a time praising my essays, although her standard of assessment was very high, and Mrs Soshil Sarojini had said, 'Heaven be praised! Gulnar has outdone herself this time. What wonderful answers! I read and reread this paper countless times.' She never had problems praising me in front of the teachers and other girls, nor did Miss Kamla Bai. Apart from the lady teachers, the male professors would also praise my intelligence and capability! The only exception was Miss Fence, who would never use a single word of praise. Perhaps she thought it below her dignity. Hunh!

And how I wanted her to appreciate my beauty! Not all the time, but sometimes impulsively, I would have liked a 'Gulnar! How beautiful you are!' At least once she could have let out a 'Today you're looking very beautiful, Gulnar,' or 'This sari really suits you.' How I would strive on the days we had a class with her to wear the saris that suited me, style my hair with care and wear colourful bangles. I was specially proud of my wrists and fingers and would place my hands on the table in such a way that Miss Fence would have a perfect view of the bangles fitting snugly on my wrists as well as of my fingers. It was quite evident that she considered me beautiful, otherwise she would not have stared so. And every time I felt that I was looking particularly good I could see she was paying me special attention. Her eyes would be fixed on me. So be it. Did she think I was made of stone or was a lifeless painting only to receive silent admiration? After all, I was a human being. A young seventeen-year-old girl, romantic and emotional! Would her precious hoard of praise have been depleted if she had said something aloud? Granted she was a professor, but Mrs Soshil was a professor as well. Did she not praise my looks?

The day I was to take part in a play which portrayed Queen Nur Jahan's love of dance and music, how Mrs Soshil had admired me while doing the make-up. 'Gulnar! You are the most appropriate person to play Nur Jahan. How well you write! Mr Soshil sings your praises. He has also been your teacher, hasn't he?' After having applied powder, lipstick, rouge, she said, 'Now lift your eyes. Let me make them up as well,' and when I did, 'Heavens! What beautiful eyes!' How I wished that instead of Mrs Soshil it had been Miss Fence who spoke those words! Why had I never cared for Mrs Soshil? What was so special about Miss Fence?

Zarina never tired of praising my eyes! And Lalita! She even wrote verses in praise of them! Zini also used to say, 'Gulnar, you must not wear glasses, they hide your beautiful eyes!' All of them would shower me with admiration. I took special care of my eyes so that Miss Fence might look into them and in her class I would take my glasses off although I had quite a problem making out what was written on the board. Hunh! Did it ever have any effect on the insensible one? But Parvaiz! Parvaiz's discerning eyes will, at first glance, respond to the beauty in mine. They will lift of their own accord. 'Your eyes! Your gazelle eyes! How black! How intoxicating!'

In college I only participated in plays so that Miss Fence should notice me. *Saint Joan* had been selected as the college play and I was to play Joan. I was so elaborately attired that even I was quite taken aback at my own image in the mirror and broke out laughing, thinking, would Joan, a village girl and a prisoner in court, have been all dressed up? But here in films and plays the paramount consideration is that the girl who plays the heroine must be lovely to look at and wear beautiful costumes. It was not the fault of Mrs Soshil and Miss Jones who had made me up for the part. Miss Jones had made me put on her khaki riding habit, and my long hair had been pinned up and left loose on the shoulders. It had not been combed but was in artful disarray on the brow and forehead. The fault had been Veedhi's; she had played the part of the Duke of York. She had been applying lipstick when it was time for the curtain to go up. Seizing my hand as I went by, she had pulled me to her: 'Gulnar! What's this! You're the heroine! No rouge, no lipstick!' She quickly put some lipstick on my lips and rubbed some rouge on my cheeks. As I glanced at the mirror in passing, I froze. How good even my dry and dishevelled hair looked! I was certain Miss Fence would praise me today. In fact she would have no option but to do so.

At the end of the play Mrs Soshil, Miss Jones and Mrs Daniels came running up on the stage and clasped my hand warmly, congratulating me on acquitting myself well in a difficult role. Everyone was electrified by my performance. All this praise, but what about Miss Fence? She hadn't even sat in the audience to see the play but had stood backstage directing the actors. I had begged her to sit in the audience for the performance, gripping her shoulders and looking at her beseechingly. If I had been in her place I would have melted. Even a stone would have more feeling.

'Gulnar! I have taken some responsibilities upon myself which I must fulfil.'

Your hallowed responsibilities! Well, at least she had viewed it from the wings.

That night I had been delayed returning to the hostel. Girls had crowded round me at every step. 'Gulnar! You did brilliantly! How can one praise your performance!' 'How beautiful you looked on stage, Gulnar!' Rescuing myself from the girls I arrived exhausted at the hostel. Zarina was outside waiting for me. She ran and embraced me. 'My dear Gulnar! You should have your hair cut and make yourself up the way you did for the play. You looked like a fairy tonight, but your make-up was not appropriate for Joan, was it? When the Inquisitor said, "Joan, you look very pale today," your cheeks were blushing like dawn!' Both of us burst into laughter. Arm in arm we ran into the dining room. All the girls had sat down to their meal. They showered me with compliments as I entered. I went to bed delighted that night but couldn't get to sleep. Hunh! What did I care for everyone's praise? Tomorrow I will meet my Miss Fence. My Angelina. And she will praise me.

The next morning I went to see her with heightened hopes, such expectations. And what did I receive from my Angelina? A deadpan face and anaemic conversation . . . Zarina was right when she said, 'Gulnar, a romantic girl like you and the insensible and frigid Miss Fence . . . you don't match. You are fire and she is ice . . .' She was truly devoid of emotion. A feelingless corpse. A stone statue. A lump of ice! How could she be compared to Parvaiz! Every vein in my Parvaiz's body courses with life. He is electric. Even in the photograph he looks so romantic.

I also managed to steal a glance at him the day that *Abba* had invited him to dinner to give him his engagement present. Zarina was over and Jabeen as well. '*Dulha Bhai* is here,' Zubeida had announced and how my heart had raced! Zarina and Jabeen had run to the window and dragged me along. 'Get up, Gulnar! Have a look at your *dulha* as well.' First I hesitated, but I was longing to catch a glimpse of him. 'What will *Ammi* say?' 'Oh, come on! Get up! Don't lose this golden opportunity.' Zarina succeeded in dragging me over to the window. How shyly he stood in front of *Abba*. When he entered the hall I tried to peep through the keyhole but the wretched keyholes were too small! We finally came up with a plan. Jabeen turned out the light in our room so that no one would be able to see inside and Zarina silently slid the bolt and opened the door a fraction. Then of course Jabeen and Zarina rushed forward . . . I don't know why I held back.

'What a handsome youth, Gul!' Zarina embraced me emotionally. I lowered my eyes shyly. 'My Gul! What a wonderful couple you make,' she said tilting my face up, love dripping from her eyes. She resumed her peeping. 'What a handsome figure and such beautiful eyes! Come here, Gul! Afraid of *Ammi* indeed!' Zarina started dragging me again. 'Have you seen your Parvaiz's eyes? A true answer to your own . . . Yes, I saw everything. The beautiful face. The laughing lips. The beautiful eyes brimming with life and impulsiveness. '*Arri*, he looks very romantic, Gul. I bet he'll go mad over you. I'll tell you from now, Gul, he'll spoil you rotten, wear you like a necklace round his neck.' I was burning with desire. I have fallen into his arms . . . Crazy . . .

'Mad woman, dying over Miss Fence. What hopes you had of that stony, emotionless woman. The same coldness and the same dull eyes in happiness and sorrow, anger or impatience! Look at Parvaiz, what an expressive face he has! As if rays of light are bursting forth . . .' Yes, he did appear the embodiment of impulsiveness. His eyes were darting around. Why? Perhaps he is seeking me out.

I wanted to break down the doors. Forgetting everyone's presence, I wanted to go and stand before him. What if I had been standing behind a curtain and the curtain had shifted for a moment and I had smiled pertly at him and then shyly lowered my eyes and left him breathless? I had been looking so charming in the blue georgette sari with the golden border.

Why should I go out in this sari? I'll wear the georgette sari brought by my Parvaiz. I pulled off the sari I had just put on and called out to Zakia who was going out with a dish of *samosas*.

'Zakia, please get me my blue sari. The georgette one.'

'All right, I'll get it, but come quickly. *Ammi* was saying she's not going to sit down with Miss Fence at the meal. It would be better if you took her place.'

I looked carelessly at the room. Miss Fence was sitting, hands clasped, looking up. Emotionless, dull eyes. Extremely thin, pale lips, sallow, pock-marked complexion. Suddenly her marks appeared to be increasing, becoming deeper and spreading all over. Her face was becoming repulsive. I quickly shook my head to rid it of the picture etched on it. It was replaced by another burgeoning image. Of Parvaiz. Those beautiful blue eyes, large, almond-shaped, intoxicating, long thick lashes. That face, the broad, beautiful forehead . . . And the lips? How beautifully they were chiselled. Luscious, full and with a slight uptilt as if they were made for smiling. That dusky complexion. Beautiful Shyam. My Shyam and I his Radha. I picked up Parvaiz's picture from the table and kissed it in a fever of impatience. 'This sari?' Alarmed, I put down the picture. Zakia was standing with the sari. 'Yes, that one.'

'*Apa,* come quickly. The *samosas* are growing cold and here you are changing sari after sari. How come you're so unconcerned while there is Miss Fence going on and on about Gulnar?'

'I'm coming.'

I picked up the picture again and forgetting everything, lost myself in its beauty. What a good-natured face. Oh, those lips. My eyes would first turn to the lips. These lips and . . . what a thought . . . I melted with shame. I put down the picture and began putting on the sari . . . What charm there was in his personality, what manliness! Compact body. Good height. Broad chest. Long, strong arms. In those arms. *Uf,* these thoughts again. There was electricity pounding through my veins, my heartbeat had increased! And the blood, it was boiling, spreading warmth. Fire. Oh, the crowding emotions, this storm! I fell on my bed and hid my face in the pillows. This . . . how delicious it was.

'Gulnar, what has come over you?'

Ammi was standing there, her face burning with anger.

'Miss Fence has been waiting for you for such a long time. Don't you have any consideration for an older person, and then she is your teacher as well,' *Ammi* went out muttering to herself.

'She's waiting for you.' 'She's calling you.' 'She's going on and on about you.'

All right, I'll go out. Yes, why not? I'll definitely go out. Wearing the sari that was brought me by my Parvaiz. Yes, and I'll wear the ring that is a sign of our engagement. I took out a small velvet box. What a beautiful ring. My engagement ring. The first letter of Parvaiz's name had been beautifully chiselled on it. How the single green gem sparkled in the midst of the white ones. I looked at it with pride and put it on. Yes, I'll go out like this and I'll tell her how happy I am about my wedding. She must be thinking I'm ashamed of my behaviour towards her, that I'll approach her wearing a sad expression, a sorry face, and that I'll relate my condition in pained tones. My suffering! Perhaps I'll cry! How I'll amaze her! On seeing my sari she'll exclaim, 'What a beautiful sari!' And I'll answer with pride, 'Parvaiz brought it.' And I'll talk about Parvaiz. Joyfully, I'll tell her how handsome Parvaiz is. I'll insist on her attending my wedding . . . I'll tell her how much I love Parvaiz. She'll burn up when she hears that. Won't she? Indeed she will. That time when I went home without taking leave she had inquired again and again, 'Gulnar, you're not getting married, are you?' When I had denied it she hadn't believed me. 'You're hiding it from me, Gulnar.' That is why she didn't congratulate me on receiving the news of my engagement . . . and now seeing on my face not sorrow but this abundance of pleasure, happiness and expectation, how she will burn up! Hunh! If she burns up, she burns up. Does it matter a whit, even if she burns to a cinder? In passing, I picked up Parvaiz's picture.

Translated by Samina Rahman

Mumtaz Shirin

Descent

He looked up.

A long flight of stairs led up, broad, white and shining. White stairs leading to the white rooms upstairs, which were bathed in light – the light up there.

They stood at the feet of the stairs. He and she. He looked up at the long flight . . . No, she couldn't go up. She couldn't climb all these steps in her condition. He said tenderly, 'Let me carry you.'

She blushed and shook her head. 'No . . . no. Fancy carrying me all the way up, and people looking on.'

'I don't care.' He stretched his arms towards her. But she pushed them aside protesting, 'I can go up the stairs myself.'

'All right then, I'll just hold you for support.'

He put his arm round her shoulders and held her tight.

Together they climbed the stairs, step by step.

The steps, broad, white, shining, led up to the white room upstairs. There was light up there, where life was born.

Pain shot through her, now, at short intervals. A few steps up and the pain became more intermittent and more severe, through her spine, her hips, her belly. Cold shivers ran down her whole body, beads of perspiration stood out on her forehead. He took out a handkerchief and mopped her face. 'It will be over soon,' he murmured tenderly. He held her close. 'Just lean on me, put all your weight on me. There, that's right. It will ease you.' She closed her eyes and let her head fall on his shoulder.

Step by step they came up.

The nurses took her in; he was asked to wait outside. Outside, he sat on a bench; it all seemed so sudden. He hadn't expected it – it was rather early. She had been all right that evening. He came home as usual, dead tired, and she greeted him with a tender, soothing smile. She was pained to see him dispirited and worn out. As usual she brought the pitcher and poured water as he washed his face and hands. What a dutiful wife! Feelings of love and gratitude surged up in his heart. He wished her to sit by him and talk to him, talk to him of the old happy days. But she said he should have his supper first; he looked so weak and exhausted. She laid the supper. He and the children sat down to their meagre meal. She went into the kitchen, perhaps to see if there was anything else to give them, and then – he saw her clutch the door and sink onto the threshold. He left his food and ran to her. He picked her up and carried her to the bed. He asked her anxiously what the matter was. But she wouldn't tell him. It was always so with her. She tried to conceal her pain from him. But he could feel her pain. And then she had to tell him that 'it' had started. He rushed her there.

He hoped all would be well – how she had shivered in his arms as he brought her up the stairs. She must be suffering so terribly. She was so weak. There was hardly any strength left in her. Would she come out alive from this life and death struggle? Pain gripped his heart as he sat there outside, waiting.

And she lay there, in the labour ward. The pains were now unbearable. Her eyes bulged out; she bit her lips hard. But she didn't moan, she didn't let a cry escape her lips. For he would know by her moaning that she was suffering terribly and he would suffer, too. She didn't utter a sound; she just suffered and suffered until she could suffer no more. She lost consciousness.

He stood by the closed door. A madness had taken possession of him. He paced up and down; then he came back and sat on the bench, fidgeting restlessly. He stared into empty space with eyes that seemed not to see. But he strained his ears hard to catch a moan, a cry from the labour ward. Not a sound could be heard from there. All was still. Did it mean . . .? He was stabbed in the heart. 'O, God, God! Let her live just this once.' He prayed silently from the depth of his soul. They said that while a new life was being born out of her, the mother's own life was nearly extinguished. He strained his ears again. All was still as before. Maybe she was bearing with it patiently. She had borne it patiently, always. Maybe she was alive, she was all right.

He sat on the bench, waiting; waiting endlessly, it seemed. Time stood still. The suffering, the pain, the torture of a lifetime was wrung into those few moments.

And, inside, she lay still unconscious. It was a very tiny baby. Before the cord was cut from its navel, it was no more. Slowly, she gained consciousness. She didn't ask about the baby. Some hidden, unknown, vague feeling, the 'sixth sense', had warned her it was dead. The nurses comforted her. She shouldn't worry; it was always so with babies born in the eighth month. They rarely lived. A nurse brought the baby and held it for her to see. Slowly, she turned her head sideways. Just a look at that tiny pale face, tiny lifeless body, and two silent tears flowed down her cheeks. And the warm flow of motherly love that had surged up in her breast anew froze within her.

The door opened and a nurse came out. He jumped to his feet and stared madly at the nurse. The nurse told him the baby had died as soon as it was born. He shouldn't worry – it was always so with babies born in the eighth month. But he wasn't thinking of the baby. Only if she were alive . . . Was she? The nurse went on, 'You shouldn't worry, you see, these babies rarely live.' 'My wife?' 'Your wife? Well, get her a cup of coffee. It will revive her a bit.'

Coffee for his wife? So she was alive.

When he brought the coffee, he saw that she had been taken to another ward. She lay there quietly on the bed. He stood by her and watched her pale, weak body.

'How are you feeling now?' he asked her softly, taking her cold, perspiring hand in his.

She smiled faintly. 'I'm all right. But this time I'm too weak, you know. Every joint in my body aches.'

They didn't speak of the baby. He thought it was better so. She was saved and that was all he had wished for.

The next morning he went to the hospital. He took the children with him too. She smiled at them. The children gathered round their mother's bed and he sat by her, holding her hand in his.

She caught the anxious look in his eyes and pressed his hand reassuringly. Her eyes rested on his face. There was a wealth of tenderness and affection in them – love, devotion and silent worship.

They had no physical attraction left: either of them. His loose, clumsy clothes dangled about his dark, bony form. She wore coarse, discoloured clothes. She had lost her figure having borne many children. They were both worn out by hard work. They had no looks. Poverty had snatched away what little charm youth had given them. Once wheat-brown, he had turned quite dark now. His cheeks had sunk in. She had a very pale yellow complexion, dark rings around her eyes sunk deep into their sockets. Hardly twenty-five, she looked aged already. She was just wasting away.

There was something other than beauty, a force stronger than physical attraction that had drawn them so together.

The elders had joined their hands according to religious rites and from then on they belonged to each other. And she knew she ought to love her husband. He was her lord, she should worship him, and she loved him, worshipped him and devoted her life to his service.

And he was aware that a weak, delicate being was given to his care, that he should protect her and support her. This weak being would share her life with him, she would be the mistress of his house, the mother of his children. And thus their hearts came together. Long communion had tended to make them what they were; it had deepened their affection and love for each other. And the children born of their love cemented the bond.

The children could feel, too, that all was not well with their mother. Anxiously they inquired, 'Mother, are you not well?' They felt her forehead. 'Is it fever?' And the youngest one said so touchingly,

'Where is it that you are feeling pain, Mum? Show me. I will kiss there and the pain will go . . .' He kissed her arms.

'Here.' She seized her little one and clasped him to her heart. She felt so very, very happy. How they loved her, her little ones, her own flesh of her flesh, blood of her blood. She had given them her lifeblood to make them grow. These little beings who had taken their shape and their life within her womb. She sighed as she thought she had not created life this time.

After all, what else was there in her dreary, miserable life? – poverty, starvation, misery, grief, pain but for the children who loved her, the husband who cared for her. Yes, this was the treasure of her life.

The visitors' time was up and they had to leave.

She followed them with her eyes as they passed out of the door of her ward.

The next morning he found her lying quiet and calm. But she was paler than ever. Her face was yellow, as if turmeric water had been sprinkled on it. It looked as though all the blood had been sucked from her body.

A nurse came in and, pricking her thumb, took a drop of blood. Absorbing it on a paper, she examined the percentage of haemoglobin in her blood. The lady doctor came in just at that time and examined it too.

The doctor turned almost furiously on him. 'Can't you see the danger your wife is in?' She went on in English, 'Can you imagine that? You never gave her liver extract injections, never gave her tonics during pregnancy. And when she is beyond all hope of recovery, you bring her here. And I suppose you will blame us for her death.'

Every word of the lady doctor fell like a hammer stroke on his heart. He did not love his wife? He did not care for her? He never gave her tonics and injections? A petty clerk: how could he afford tonics and injections for his wife? And she was reduced to this condition. She was near death . . . near death . . . Oh, hell is poverty.

He no longer went by bus to his office, but walked all the way. He stopped smoking his cheap cigarettes. And with the few annas that he saved, he bought fruit. He borrowed money and paid for her injections.

But she lay there pale and weak as ever, a most deathly pale. Her face was bleached white. Her body was cold and numb. Warm leather gloves and stockings were drawn on her hands and legs. Hot-water bottles and bags were kept under her feet. One could feel the presence of something invisible hovering over her. Some foreboding of death.

Yet she had a faint, reassuring smile for him. As he sat by, looking at her, pain reflected in his eyes. He comforted her: 'You'll get well. I'll take good care of you. I'll give you tonics and fruit. I'm saving money, you know.'

And very sadly she smiled at him: 'Yes, I'll get well' – a ray of hope.

Maybe this hope would keep her candle of life still burning. But the next moment he realized that her smile was a forced smile, her eyes had a faraway look.

And then came the critical night. Her calm gave way to groans. That night she moaned and groaned ceaselessly, piteously. He saw the crisis coming. He begged the nurses and doctors to let him stay with her that one night. They didn't listen to his entreaties. That was against the hospital rules! Moreover, it wasn't a special ward that anybody could be allowed to stay with the patient! A nurse came in and gave her tablets for sleep, shouting at her brutally, 'Can't you be quiet? You're groaning horribly. Don't you realize the patients in other wards are being disturbed?'

The patients in the 'other wards'. Why couldn't she come out with the whole truth? The patients in the 'special wards', 'the chosen few' – and this treatment was meted out to him because he was poor, he was not of 'the chosen few', he thought bitterly as he trotted home. Her groans haunted him. And as he lay wide awake, staring at the ceiling, he could hear that piteous moaning all night long.

Next morning she was calm again. Did it mean that the crisis was over?, he thought hopefully. But the lady doctor examined her and shook her head in despair. 'There's only one hope left.'

'What is it, doctor?' he asked madly.

'Blood transfusion . . .'

'Please examine my blood, doctor. If it suits her . . .'

And the doctor looked at this man from head to foot. Would he give his blood, this lean, lanky man? He seemed to have very little of it himself. But his beseeching, melting look seemed to answer: he would. 'I would give any quantity of my blood, if it could save her life.'

A few hundred cubic centimetres of blood were drawn from his body and transfused into hers. As her husband's blood, every drop of which contained the warmth of his love, passed through her veins, she gained a little warmth. She seemed to revive. He touched her head. It was warm, it was warm. He bent over her and whispered softly, 'You will recover now, surely.'

She gave him a warm smile, she had understood everything. She thanked him with her eyes and she opened her lips to say something. Her lips trembled; she turned blue and her whole body passed through violent convulsions so that it shook all over. She dug her nails in the sheets. He caught hold of her and bent over her. She wanted to say something, but her lips just parted and trembled. Perhaps she was asking for her children. In his dismay, this thought flashed through his mind. He asked the female neighbours, who had come along with him, to go and get the children. Their house was not far off. They were soon brought there. She looked at them one by one. She tried to stretch her arms out towards the youngest one but her arms fell, lifeless. She looked at him for the last time, as though she were bidding him goodbye.

And then all was over.

Beating his head, he called out her name again and again. But soon he realized he was in the hospital. He shouldn't behave like this. And then there were the children. He should keep calm in front of them. He let himself fall on a chair. The children stood by their father's chair and stared at the body of their mother – the mystery of death was beyond their understanding.

He sat staring at her, too, as the nurses were covering her with white sheets. White sheets, and a face as white as those sheets. White face and thick black hair falling on her shoulders. He stared and stared.

He was oblivious to his surroundings. Faintly, very faintly, he caught a few words that were being spoken around him. It was the lady doctor who was saying, 'It's too late at night. You may take the body home tomorrow. Meanwhile the corpse will be laid in the mortuary. We're sorry we couldn't save her life . . . and you can pay the bill later . . .'

And the depressed-class women, who bore the corpses down, were shrieking, 'We shan't take it down unless we're paid first.'

And he heard the nurses saying to each other, 'After all, we've seen so many deaths here, it never gave us a fright to see a dead body. We're used to it. But look at her. Don't you feel . . .?' They whispered something.

They were insulting her even in death.

Suddenly he got up and lifted the body in his arms. Somebody brought forward the stretcher. He pushed it aside. And passing by all who stood staring at him astonished and shocked, he carried her body to the stairs leading down to the back yard.

A few days back – how many days was it? – he had brought her up the stairs, supporting her, holding her tight. He had made her ascend the stairs and now, bearing her lifeless body in his arms, he was going down.

There was life in this body once. Why, even a few moments ago. Now it was cold and stiff and heavy in death. He had loved this body, loved it for ten years, and now she was lost to him for ever. How often had he carried this body in his arms when it was light and soft and warm? She was hardly fourteen when she came to him as a bride. His mother was alive then. She made her work all day. When his mother was out visiting relatives, they had a gay time. He would lift her in his arms and whirl her round. Those happy days had come to an end too soon. Hard work and childbearing had made her very weak; she was constantly ill. He asked her not to work so hard, but she wouldn't listen to him. When she was at her work, he would go behind her stealthily, lift her up gently and lay her on her bed so that she might rest. Yes, so often. And now he was bearing this body in his arms for the last time.

He was bearing her down; down the stairs.

The stairs were narrow and dark. There was darkness all about him. The darkness of night, the darkness of death. The steps seemed never-ending. A long way down . . . down, down. A long descent. The last descent.

Translated by the author

Razia Fasih Ahmed

The Inferno

'Thirty years, for thirty years my mother kept burning in this inferno and is still here.' Nasir's hands were trembling and his face was pale with emotion and stress.

'I've not been with her since the day of my birth, although she is only a few paces away from me! Have you ever heard of anything like that before? Tell me, tell me.' Nasir's voice grew more fierce and hoarse as he demanded an answer from Aijaz, although he wasn't really conscious of what he was saying.

Aijaz felt helpless. Nasir advanced towards him to console him in some way. He placed his head on his friend's shoulder and broke into tears. He wept like a child until he was over his anguish and felt somewhat relieved. Then he lifted his head from Aijaz's shoulder and looked at his friend, ashamed and puzzled as a child. Before Aijaz could utter a word, Nasir moved towards the window and seated himself beside it on a chair, drowned in thoughts.

Aijaz had come to Nasir's place to spend his summer vacation with him. Nasir's village was the most beautiful place he had ever seen. It was situated in a valley by a torrential river, surrounded by emerald green grass and colourful wild flowers. A range of high mountains overlooked the valley and gave the village an entrapped but pretty look. Nasir's father was the lord of all the land nearby besides being the owner of a few sugar mills. He was not only rich but also the soul and master of every person and thing in his land. He was the king and commander in his estate. According to the local custom he had separate abodes for men and women. The men's quarters, along with the guest suites, were designed by highly qualified architects and built by engineers. They had all the modern facilities, while the women lived in old dark buildings made of stone and mud and surrounded by a high wall which had only one huge gate through which no male over the age of twelve could pass without permission. It was in this area that the pets and farm animals had their thatched houses.

Aijaz wanted to say something but did not know what to say. Then he remembered a photograph that he had found in one of the books on the shelf. He went and took the photo from the book.

'Look at this picture. Have you seen a prettier face?' asked Aijaz.

Nasir glanced at it disconcertedly; then suddenly he snatched the picture from Aijaz and looked at it closely.

'How did you get it?' he asked excitedly.

'I found it in one of the old poetry books which bear the name of Qudsia. Do you know anybody by this name?'

'I've never seen my mother or her picture,' said Nasir ignoring his friend's question, 'but this can only be her picture. Oh, what beauty, what grace!' His eyes were filled with tears and he pored over the picture lovingly, rapturously.

'Is her name Qudsia, by any chance?'

'Yes, you silly!', Nasir smiled, still looking at the picture.

'Nasir, now I can see a great resemblance between you and her,' said Aijaz.

'Don't be ridiculous,' Nasir said impatiently. The idea of his resembling his mother was almost sacrilegious to him because at the time his mother had risen above being human – she appeared almost divine.

Plunged into deep thought for a while, Nasir said in a whisper, 'Imagine what a great risk a foreigner must have taken in helping her, and I, her own flesh and blood, did not lift a finger to free her from this dungeon. Isn't it disgraceful? You could never know how the thought keeps torturing me.'

'You were not in a position to help her while you were just a student, but now you can. You might be able to get a house adjacent to your hospital as other doctors with families have. If you don't get it right away, my mother would be only too glad to take her in until you have your own place.'

Nasir did not answer but remained engulfed in his thoughts. Aijaz walked up to the door from where he could see the cliff overhanging the river, which made a natural ledge, transformed into an excellent terrace by the builders. Nasir's father, the elder Khan, had his meetings there with servants, farmers and business supervisors. He was there right then, sitting on a wooden *takht* covered with expensive chintz cloth, an enormous round pillow behind his back. The day Aijaz arrived, the Khan greeted him cordially and gave orders to entertain him in the best possible manner. His big Chevrolet, the Land Rover, a jeep, the horses and the boats were put at his disposal. That was why Aijaz had come to think the Khan to be a very kind and generous man. But now he knew that it was only the Khan's vanity and chauvinism expressing itself in this way.

The two young men had taken advantage of his offer. They had covered long distances on fishing and shooting sprees. At first Aijaz was afraid of riding a horse but soon he got over the fear. The horses were so tame and trained, and moved with such assurance and composure, that even a child could ride them.

In the beginning when Nasir told him strange stories about superstitions, illnesses and their treatments, Aijaz hardly believed him, but now he had witnessed so many incredible incidents that he started believing in the tales. He had seen seven demons possessing a girl; seen them exorcized one by one by a mullah. He had come to understand the psychology of the inhabitants. Being associated with high mountains, a man was bound to be rugged and harsh. Living in a place where tumultuous rivers carve their way, where fierce blizzards rage, human feelings are apt to become reckless. Where the comforts are so rare and nature is man's friend as well as his foe, it is not unusual to have complicated feelings. Aijaz had seen a queer mixture of opposites in Nasir, who was an Afreedi Pathan. They could be fast friends and fierce enemies at the same time. They could be very affectionate, companionable and hospitable if one knew how to handle them, but if by mistake one touched the wrong key, they could become extremely ill-humoured and cranky. Aijaz knew by now that, in spite of his spirited nature, Nasir was very tender at heart.

Aijaz was slowly coming to understand Nasir but there were still a few things about him which appeared odd to him. Nasir would suddenly get lost in deep thought, as if he were not there at all. Strangely, unlike most of the boys, he would not show any interest in girls or talk seriously about marriage. In his own home he seldom went to the part of the house where the women lived. One day Aijaz had asked the reason for this and Nasir had replied that it was not considered discreet to be always visiting the women's quarters. Besides, though there were lots of cousins, aunts and other womenfolk, by not seeing them often he had left a communication gap, so that there was not a single common topic to talk about.

'What about your mother?' asked Aijaz. The moment he uttered the last word he realized his mistake and knew what was coming. Nasir had once told him never to ask any questions about his mother.

'Sorry,' Aijaz said apologetically, 'you had asked me not to mention your mother, but that was in the days when we were mere room-mates. Now we are friends and I share with you everything which happens in my family, don't I?'

Nasir kept looking at him with an intent eye but said nothing.

'I think I have a right to know whether your mother is alive or, God forbid, she is dead. Even if she belongs to a family which people regard as defamed . . .'

'Shut up! Don't you say another word,' Nasir shouted and leapt towards Aijaz as if he were going to strike him. But he suddenly stopped and went out of the room slamming the door behind him.

Aijaz felt resentful and angry. After all, what had he said to send Nasir into such a frenzy? He knew that women of inferior status were often taken into the households of the rich. If Nasir was born of such a mother, it was all the more laudable that the elder Khan treated him as his first-born – as if born of his first lady wife – and had given him all the privileges of a highborn son. So far as Aijaz was concerned, it did not make any difference whether his mother was the darling daughter of a lord or only a milkmaid. Aijaz felt so bitter that he decided to pack and leave.

When Nasir returned to Aijaz's room he saw him packing.

'What are you doing?' he asked rather curtly.

Aijaz preferred not to answer. This hurt and outraged Nasir more than an answer would have done.

'All right, go! But never call yourself my friend again or talk of friendship for that matter.' There was something in his voice which made Aijaz look up. He saw a very wretched person standing there. Nasir's face looked as if the blood had drained out of his body. His eyes were red as though he had been crying.

'Do you believe in heaven and hell?' he asked.

'Yes I do,' Aijaz said, still looking at his face which looked stranger than ever.

'I don't know what concept of hell you have,' Nasir said solemnly. 'Just imagine your mother there in flesh and blood till all eternity. Can you do that?' he said, staring at Aijaz in a strange way.

Nasir's look, more than his words, made Aijaz shudder. He had never seen Nasir look or talk like that before. Nasir's face was chalk white; he was trembling and his hand swelled with the tight grip he had on the door.

'I'm sorry, I didn't know anything about that.' Aijaz let the shirt he was folding drop back on the bed and sat down. Nasir went to his room, coming back after a few minutes with an old notebook in his hand. 'This is my mother's diary and I want you to read it. It has not been read by anyone other than me. Remember it's sacred to me and I expect you never to tell its contents to anybody. If you can promise that, I'll let you see it.'

'I promise,' said Aijaz and held his hand out to take the notebook.

'Then go ahead and read it.' Nasir handed the notebook to him and left.

That was how Aijaz came to know the story of the mother's captivity in her own house.

While looking at the magnificent view outside, Aijaz started fantasizing about what he had read in Qudsia's diary.

A British tourist, John, whom Nasir had referred to as the foreigner, must have been sitting at the foot of the hill with a line cast in the cerulean blue water of the stream to catch fish. He surely must have been fascinated by the cold, transparent water through which coloured pebbles could be seen as clearly as they are seen through glass. The light breeze must have tossed the long grass and the fragile orange and purple coloured poppies. He must have felt very elevated and lighthearted with rolling clouds in the sky, the whole atmosphere so charged with beauty, and he sitting there with a basketful of snacks and a flask of hot tea.

A little distance away, maids with their heads covered discreetly with white embroidered *dupattas* might have been busy filling their vessels with water to carry to the Khan's house. Among them, wrapped up just like her maidservant, would be Nasir's mother who, being a lady of the house, was not supposed to go out at all except on very special occasions such as a wedding or a death in the family, and that, too, in a covered cart. She had found it impossible to abide by the rules because she was born and raised in quite a different environment. She had been educated in a convent school where she had read Wordsworth, Shelley, and so on, and had acted in many English plays. She had been very fond of swimming and playing tennis, and even ballroom dancing.

So, as a last resort, she started going out in the disguise of a maidservant and met the man who vowed to save her.

Aijaz enjoyed visualizing him in a broad-brimmed hat to keep off the sun, writing something occasionally in his diary which lay beside him on the grass. Then on a sudden impulse he got up and started walking towards the women. Aijaz almost saw him with his beard and all, his jeans rolled up to his knees showing his well-shaped legs.

He came to the women and started talking to them in their own language, which surprised and amused them. He soon turned his attention to the woman who sat with her beautiful feet in the water, turning her head away, pretending not to see him. He did not like being ignored, so weighing his options cautiously, he went to her and said, '*Salaam aleikum.*'

'*Wa 'leikum asalaam,*' she said in a voice hardly more than a whisper and pulled her *dupatta* down to her forehead, then over her eyes.

He kept staring at her, then asked, 'Who are you?'

She hesitated for a moment, then answered, 'I am a maidservant at the Khan's house.'

'Really!' He seemed amused. 'What do you do?'

'I work there as all these women do,' she said.

'But I have seen you doing nothing all this time while these women were washing clothes and carrying the water to the house.'

'It's my day off,' she said and smiled in spite of herself.

'Come on,' he laughed, 'the servants haven't days off – not even *Eid* day.' Then he said in English, 'If you are the Khan's wife and have come here for an outing, I see no harm in it. Don't be afraid of me. I rather appreciate your ingenuity and am one hundred per cent with you.'

At that moment she threw all precaution to the wind and started talking to him in English. She told him that her position in the Khan's house was exactly that of a bird in a cage.

'You are not happy, I presume,' he said.

'Just as happy as a caged bird is,' she said.

All of a sudden the smile vanished from Aijaz's face. Looking very concerned, Nasir said, 'I've made up my mind!'

'What's that?'

'Let's start immediately.' He took Aijaz's hand and dragged him out of the room towards the female suites. His determination knew no bounds. He passed the giant gate as if he had all authority to do so. Aijaz followed him timidly, unable to defy his friend but afraid in his heart for him and himself.

Inside the gate there was a dark, narrow corridor with huge, earthen pots containing corn, lined up on both sides of the wall. Nasir went through the corridor like a sixteenth-century warrior. Stopping at the entrance to the actual building he shouted, 'Gulshan *Dai*, come out.'

A middle-aged woman immediately came out of the house, but looked very unhappy and perplexed.

'I've come to see Mother and see her I must, do you understand?' he demanded, with the indication to the woman that he meant every word that he had uttered. 'Don't just stand there. Show me the way.'

The woman trembled as if, suddenly, a wave of cold air had caught her. She kept rubbing her hands together.

'Come, if you must,' she said, and led the way.

Nasir followed her and beckoned Aijaz to follow. They passed a labyrinth of rooms and corridors and finally reached a dark room in which a kerosene lamp was burning. With her back to the light, a tall woman was taking out something from a cupboard. Hearing the footsteps she turned around to look. They both saw her in amazement. She looked beautiful, tall and fair, like a statue in marble. She stood there, looking at Nasir, mute and motionless, as if rooted there for years.

'Mother!' Nasir whispered and bowed down a little.

She lifted him up, holding his head in both hands, hugged him and kissed him on the forehead. Then, as if not believing her eyes, she kept staring at him, fearing that he would vanish – so many times before, she had experienced this image to be an illusion or a dream.

'Mother, I want to take you to Karachi.' He noticed the terrified look of his mother and added, 'Don't be scared. I'm your son and you can go with me. I'll make all the arrangements. We'll cover some of the distance on horseback; it will shorten the journey and arouse no suspicion. Then we shall travel by car.'

'Son, this is the first time in my life that I've seen and talked to you. I beg you to say something nice and cheerful to me. Tell me about yourself; what have you been doing all these years?'

Then she saw Aijaz and a streak of fear and distrust gripped her. 'Who is he?' she asked, perplexed.

'He's a friend. You can trust him as much as you can trust me. He will be going with us. Now, you want me to tell you something nice. Is there anything better than what I have just told you? I'm going to take you out of this dungeon for ever.'

'I'm not going anywhere,' she said firmly.

'You don't mean it?' Nasir said in astonishment.

'Yes I do,' she said, 'you should realize that he cannot harm me any more than he has already done, but he can make your life miserable. He can disinherit you, deprive you of all you have and even kill you. He is capable of doing anything.'

'But I don't care and I don't believe he can harm us once we are out of his jurisdiction.' He foresaw his mother trying to persuade him again and decided to put forward his trump card. 'It's not fair, Mother!' he said, 'you were willing to go with a foreigner but are reluctant to go with me, your own son.'

At this, the soft crumpled face, smiling and crying at the same time, suddenly stiffened. Her hands remained suspended in the air. She clenched her fists and stared at Nasir as if she were in a trance. It was after quite some time that she was able to speak. 'Tell me,' she said, 'what have they told you about me? The deceitful friends! I assented to this life of unthinkable misery because they promised me not to tell my son anything about my past.'

'They haven't told me anything, Mother. I know everything because I've read your diary.' He took her hand in his and tried to comfort her but she was extremely distressed.

'Where did you find my diary?'

'Among your old books.'

'Where is it now? Did your father read it?'

'No, he didn't, and it's safe with me. Trust me, Mother!'

'Well, I was sure that it was burnt long ago. I'm surprised to hear that it's still there. I don't really remember fully what I wrote in it – it was so long ago, but I remember that I wrote only the absolute truth.'

'You don't have to say that; I believed it while I read it.' He patted her hand to comfort her.

'Did you?' she said, 'and let me tell you one thing, that besides God, you are the only one I cared to know how I felt at the time and what had really happened.'

'Oh, don't bother about the past now, we have a life ahead! Just be prepared tonight. Only take a few things with you. First, we will take the path among the hills. Can you ride a horse?'

'Yes, I can.'

'It's all settled then. I'll come for you just after midnight. I have found your picture in one of your books. May I keep it?' Nasir seemed to linger on, conversing because he simply had no heart to leave.

'Why not?' his mother said lovingly. 'Who has more right to keep it than you?'

The elderly woman who had ushered them in came to the door. It was already late and she wanted them to leave.

'Goodbye, Mother,' he said, taking hold of Qudsia's hand again and leaving, though not as fast as he had entered the house.

When he came back to his room he was in a state of euphoria. 'I feel as if I had come out from under tons of weight. I'm going to pay, at last, some of the debt I owe to my mother.' He kept saying things like that, pacing the room.

Aijaz could understand his excitement; still, he chose to give him a word of warning. 'Mind you, there are still some very hard times ahead.'

'I don't care. Just tell me, did you notice how beautiful my mother still is, how graceful and elegant! How can a man destroy such a person for his own vanity? Aren't we men mean and selfish compared to such a woman?'

'Yes, I think we are. Now what could have happened to the person who tried to free your mother? Did your father have him killed and buried some place here?'

'I don't think so. It's never easy to get a foreigner killed just like that. He must have gone back home. Now, get some sleep. I'll come back after making arrangements for the journey.' He left Aijaz in a hurry as he suddenly realized how much there was to be done.

Instead of going to sleep, Aijaz picked up Qudsia's notebook and started reading it again.

He had an old, two-door, weather-beaten Italian car with a high, oval-shaped rear window like a ventilator in an old building. The back seat and the entire rear portion of the car were cluttered with hundreds of things ranging from sleeping-bags to fishing rods, dangling at all angles. Looking in from outside, one could see no part of the back seat from any of the windows. The car, though old and battered, had a new and reliable engine. John drove the car at high speed, talking at the same time to somebody lying hidden under a heap of clothing on the back seat. He had no means of knowing whether the person he was talking to was listening to him at all because there was not the slightest response. He still continued his monologue.

'Ah! What a lovely place, a beauty not ruined by modern living. This is the real thing.' His voice had such exultation as if the cool breeze he was breathing was intoxicating. 'It's not like the places in Europe and England where hundreds of tourists swarm like bees. The promoters of tourism, who have made it an industry, charge for admission to every building, well or stone, so that one gets exasperated. Hotel bills are enormous! Here, I was treated like royalty for three weeks and was not charged a single paisa. When I insisted on making a payment, the elder Khan got red in the face: "How can you insult us like that?" he said. "Taking money from a guest! We are *zamindars*, meals for guests are ready here every day as a matter of course. People from other villages come and they are always welcome. If you had a mind to pay, you should have stayed in a hotel in a big town. You shouldn't have come here in the first place." My God! What hospitality, what values! But at the same time what atrocities! Man, slave unto man, and wives treated worse than slaves. In the West, if women had to live like that for a single day, I'm sure they would either commit suicide or kill their husbands.'

He took a deep breath and said, 'Hi there, is anybody at home? Oh, what's the matter? I'm really scared, Qudsia, are you all right?'

'I'm crying,' arose a faint voice from among the pile of clothing on the back seat.

'Oh, I'm so relieved. You're still alive! Now tell me what happened to your sense of freedom! Have you ever seen a bird crying on being set free?'

Suddenly Qudsia started laughing at the idea of a bird crying, but soon returned to her weeping.

'Look, I don't have time to stop the car, give you something to drink or wash your face. We still have a long way to go. Just tell me if, by any chance, you want to go back on your decision. Don't worry about me, just say so, and I'll go back and face the consequences.'

'No, no! For God's sake, don't talk like that! If we go back, both of us will be killed,' Qudsia said in a frightened voice.

'Then, Qudsia, dear, cheer up. We're in this together till death do us part. Have a sip from the flask, forget the past and think of the future.' John speeded up the car and stopped talking. He realized that it was naive of him to talk as if he was on a date with a girl.

Qudsia tried to think about the future but her mind was foggy. She was unable to see any future for herself. Everything was so uncertain; she was not sure of her freedom. Things had happened so fast! When she came to know that there was a person who was willing to take the risk of freeing her, she only thought that it was the chance of a lifetime. The big question which loomed upon her was: 'Now or never.' For fear of 'never', she had taken a leap into the unknown without thinking whether she would ever land on her feet alive. As much as she wanted to think about the future, her mind unwittingly dragged her into the past.

When, at the age of fifteen, she had a proposal of marriage from Shahzore Khan, mother superior of the convent school had opposed it tooth and nail. Qudsia was an exceptionally intelligent girl. Marrying her at such a tender age would ruin her, but Qudsia's father, who was a brigadier in the army, decided that she should get married to the boy. The reason was that Qudsia's mother was dead and he was suffering from lung cancer. He wanted to settle Qudsia in matrimony before he was gone. He personally went to see Shahzore's family and accepted the proposal. He told Qudsia that the family was rich and well-established. The boy was educated and handsome. The only drawback he could find was that the family was a little old-fashioned, even rustic, but it didn't matter because only some years back his own father had been as conservative and old-fashioned as anybody else. It was just a matter of time, he had consoled her.

Even then, she had not agreed to the proposal. She had told her cousins that she did not want to get married in the first place, and not to Shahzore Khan in any case. The girls told all this to their mothers, and they to their husbands, as was the custom , but nobody really took Qudsia seriously. It is not for young girls like Qudsia to decide on a life partner. Then again, naive girls often talked like that before marriage. It was considered discreet not to show eagerness about one's marriage. Everything would just turn out fine as it always does. Qudsia at one time thought to open her heart to her father, but he was too sick to be bothered. It would break his heart to see his daughter defy him as it was unheard-of in their family for a girl to go against the wishes of her elders in connection with her marriage.

So it happened that the responsible persons who came to take her formal consent to the wedding did not bother to listen to anything from her. Even before she could utter a word, her consent was taken for granted and confirmed by one of the elderly ladies already clustered at the door of the room where she sat in the midst of scores of girls and women all talking at the same time.

Soon the women were congratulating and embracing each other as the marriage was solemnized in the men's quarters. Afterwards, in the evening, she tried to explain all this to Shahzore Khan, hoping that he would understand her perfectly, but he did not want to hear a word of what she was trying to tell him. He was the one who wanted her as his wife and what mattered to him was that he had got her. From then on, the thought of being a captive never left her mind. She felt an invisible chain around her neck and felt it tightening more and more every day because Shahzore did not believe in women's liberation. He had married her in the hope that she would gradually come round to his way of thinking.

All decisions were made by the men and the women were informed only of those which concerned them. Even the beauty of the surroundings, which was admired by the whole world, was not for the eyes of their womenfolk. Money which came in heaps was not theirs to spend. Whenever she planned to go to some place, she was told that the cars were not available. They were either taken away by the Khans or were being used by their guests – usually high officials from the government. She, as a special case, was allowed to wear the clothes of her liking and was given a nice bed, a dressing-table and a bookcase, which was a rarity in the household. Other women in the family did not have these pieces of furniture in their rooms. They all lived in proximity at the mercy of their masters as long as they were needed. Thereafter, they would often contact tuberculosis or some other disease and die spitting blood or remain miserable in some other way. That was none of their master's concern.

After her marriage, Qudsia's father had gone to England for treatment. Qudsia wanted to go and see him but was not permitted by her husband to have a house built for her in Peshawar. Disgusted, she wrote a long letter to her father to explain things, but all the reply she received was a telegram from London informing her that her father had died during the operation.

Qudsia was roused from her memories at daybreak by the fragrance of the flowers in the cold morning breeze. She could tell from just a glimpse through the window that they were passing through old familiar places. She could see Amandra Rest House – a new building constructed in an old fort, so high that from the rest house one could see the miles of fertile lands, canals, mountains and zigzagging roads. She had been there often with her father. She had played chess with him and his friends and painted from its balconies the fabulous scenes of sunrise, sunset and moonlit nights. Very soon they were passing by the Malakand Fort. Qudsia had also stayed once in one of the buildings in that fort. She would never forget the night when an earthquake hit the place. They had rushed out of their bedrooms in the dark because the electricity was disrupted by the quake. After coming out of the house they were staying in, they found that the high stone fort walls and the high hills were too near and there was no escape from them; they might as well remain inside. She and her father again went inside and stayed awake a long time, sitting and talking in the sitting room. No one else stirred because of the earthquake. The people there were used to the phenomenon and knew it was better not to go out of their houses.

The next day, when they had descended from the Malakand Fort to go to Risalpur, there was a slight drizzle. A long rainbow spanning the sky with such vivid colours fascinated her. The next spectacular experience was to witness the same rainbow sprawling down in the alley. Going a little further, she noticed the second rainbow in the sky and that, too, lay flat on the earth in the valley. The phenomenon was so unique and wonderful that she asked her father to stop the car. Both of them enjoyed the two rainbows, in the sky and on the earth, for quite some time before starting again. As she recalled the dreamlike marvel, she felt sleepy. Exhausted as she was, she dozed off.

'Wake up, Qudsia,' she heard somebody whisper in her ear. When she woke, she felt someone gently slapping her cheek. For a few moments she had no idea where she was and who he was who dared to wake her up in such a rude way. She was almost outraged when, suddenly, the whole thing came to her mind as a shock. It was not a dream!

John was stroking her cheek trying to wake her up, talking at the same time. 'You can't do this to me. It's only the beginning. You have taken such a big step. You can't let things go now. You need to have courage, otherwise we could both be in danger.'

'Where are we?' Qudsia asked, sitting up in her seat.

'Listen, we are in Risalpur. This is a house of a friend. We cannot continue our journey in this car. I will leave the car here and my friend will take care of it. We will now travel in his car. I will try to change my appearance and you will have to change yours. You must wear the outfit of my friend's wife to look like an Englishwoman. Can you do that?'

'I'll do whatever you say.'

'Good girl!'

So she was in good old Risalpur!

She knew the roads, streets and lanes of the place as the lines on her hand. The roads always seemed bare. How fast she used to ride on her red bicycle along the metalled roads. The Farash trees, with their low branches, seemed to caress her head with loving hands. The green hedges and the rose bushes adorned the roads. Under the shadow of the tall trees was her convent school. She had been a favourite pupil of the teachers throughout her school-days. The part of the building where the nuns resided and had their chapel added a sense of mystery for her. So did the army mess with its huge leather sofas, heavy silver pieces and antiques like the Chinese vases from the Ming period and the tiled screen from the Mughal days. She also remembered having seen part of the flag from the Lucknow residency, a prize for the British army from the 1857 war which was considered a mutiny.

She had a sudden impulse to ride a bicycle and surprise her mother superior or her tennis coach, or go to the cemetery where her dear brother and mother were buried. Getting out of the car, she cast a look around. The houses were still the same, with big gardens and courtyards, so large that each house was a hundred yards apart. The place looked desolate, as if it were a town where dwellers were made to disappear by magic. Staggering, she went inside the house.

After taking a shower and changing into a new pair of clothes, she had a light breakfast. Then they started off again. Qudsia looked at the familiar roads with nostalgia; North Road, Broadway Road, all shaded by trees as before. There was lush green grass on the polo ground. Eucalyptus trees were waving slowly in the breeze, and big roses peeped out from in between the hedges and around the bungalows. The car passed by the army mess and Qudsia recalled that it was in this mess that Shahzore Khan had first seen her. It was a guest night and Shahzore Khan had been invited by a friend in the army. He had declared then and there that he had fallen in love at first sight with the glamorous girl in the black dress. His friends had warned him that the girl was being raised more like a Westerner than a conservative Pathan would like his wife to be. Shahzore Khan did not heed them; he was sure that after marriage she would mend her ways as a good wife should.

Whenever she complained of suffocation, he would be surprised. 'Why, what's wrong with this place?'

He pretended that he could not understand that if a place was good enough for his mother, sisters and other women relatives, why could it not be good enough for his wife? Besides, where could she go? She did not have any parental home. There was no need to leave in the summer because the weather was so cool and pleasant, and there was no need to go somewhere in the winter because they were all used to the cold weather.

'Qudsia, you told me that you love Wordsworth and I tell you that you will simply fall in love with the Lake District when you see it. It is so pleasant by the lakes at all times. The afternoons are so calm and quiet, with long shadows of trees across the grass, turning it into a beautiful hue of pale green. In the evenings the waters are so quiet that you want to hold your breath not to disturb their serenity. I don't think you would ever be able to forget the feeling you get when you see Lake Windermere at night for the first time. Qudsia, please say something.'

'I don't know. My mind is in a haze and I find it impossible to think at all.' With all that confusion, though, Qudsia was surprised how he had presumed she was going to accompany him to England.

'Till now, you've known England only through books by Galsworthy, Virginia Woolf and E. M. Forster; but when you see it with your eyes, it will be such a novel experience, a bell ringing in your head every time. Well, this is the parliament building with Big Ben at its side; this is Marble Arch, and this is the Tower!'

Qudsia smiled in spite of herself. John was not a tall, bearded man at the time, but a boy from a country who was excited at the glamour of the big city and wanted to show everything to his friend.

Then, suddenly, he changed the subject. 'Qudsia, look at these ruddy formations turned into hills spread for miles. Have you ever seen them before?'

'Yes,' she tried to say, but her voice choked. She knew the place too well. Her heart sank as she tried to huddle back in the seat, not wanting to see those bloody hills. The place was associated with the death of her mother. For her, the hills were red only because they had drunk the blood of her mother who had died here in an accident. She pretended to be asleep. She did not get up or look out till they reached Rawalpindi.

As always, Rawalpindi was a little quiet and a little noisy, a little pretty and a little ugly in places, with a bit of new but lots of old too. She had stayed in Rawalpindi with her father many times on their way to Murree. They would take a stroll on the Mall and shop in Saddar at a huge department store of bygone days when only cantonments had that kind of store. It was run by a Parsi gentleman who had migrated from Iran. She would like to know, of course, whether the store was still there. Yes, it was there; she was able to catch a glimpse of it as the car passed by, but it was not the only one now. There were more stores of the same kind, a bakery and a grocery shop. There were new buildings, schools and new roads. Yes, changes do come in life. They are more visible in cities. People like her father-in-law and her husband oppose the changes in their villages. No girl could speak Urdu, the national language, because they were not supposed to use it in any way. They had no right whatsoever. They could not have their say in any matter, especially not about their own marriage.

In spite of very severe punishments imposed by their own families, girls often took the risk and ran away with their paramours. Those who were caught had to die by the hands of their closest relatives: father, brother or uncle. She, too, was now running away with someone though not in the same sense of the word, but that would make no difference for them. People would only think that she must have been having an affair with someone and that she had found an opportunity to elope with him. They were not capable of thinking otherwise. The name of the sons of some neighbouring *zamindars* would come up, no doubt. She knew that she wouldn't select a single one of them to run away with. Her father-in-law, a clever and shrewd person, might suspect the tourist who behaved abnormally in so many ways. The police must have been informed by now and the people from their own estate must have been sent to catch them. What would happen if they found them? She did not like to think beyond that point because there was death, certain and cruel, beyond that.

She hated to think of death while she was alive. She shook her head in order to do away with the thoughts that disturbed her. Raising her head a little out of the heap of things surrounding her, she looked out. The wheat plants only a few inches high in the North West Frontier Province were two feet tall in the Punjab. There were villages along the road and the atmosphere there was as calm and quiet as ever. The monotonous sound of the Persian wheel run by the mundane circling of oxen with bands on their eyes, the usual fluttering of the fowl and the routine humdrum of human voices were all mixed in the surroundings. In the midst of everyday life their car was rolling fast to an unknown destination, to a place of which neither she nor her fellow traveller had a clear idea.

Why not go to her mother's relatives in Karachi? They were educated and lived in a big city; they would understand the terrible situation she was in! But what if they didn't and secretly informed her husband about her whereabouts? Well, Karachi was still far off and she could decide later. At present they had just reached Lahore, the capital city of the province of the Punjab, where she had lived with her parents when she was a little girl.

She remembered Lahore as if she had seen it in a dream. She had no idea of time and space, no concept of how old she was at the time, which building was situated where, or how far one place was from her home or from any other place. But all that she remembered was colourful and beautiful, though hazy as seen through a mist. One afternoon they had taken her to a big park where they had stayed till dusk; she had seen fireflies glowing in the trees, twinkling like hundreds of lamps flying down to the grass and then flying back again to the trees.

Her mother and father would both go to the club in the evening, and her nanny would take her for a stroll to a nearby park where there were many other children and their nannies. At times they would walk along the sidewalk of the Mall on their way to the big store from which she would buy chocolates. She loved the shade of the trees – a kind of tunnel made by them coming up from both sides of the road and interlocking at the top. She had a strong feeling of being able to see that road now, but she knew she could not indulge in that kind of a whim. Still, the past would not leave her alone. She had one other memory. There was a big fort and in one of the rooms there were tiny pieces of coloured glass studded all over the walls and the ceiling, making fabulous patterns of birds, peacocks, grapes in a bowl and beautiful gimlets. The guide who was showing them the fort had lighted a torch and had swirled it around, lifting it high up in the air, and the whole room had glittered and glimmered with the innumerable tiny lights twinkling like stars. She came to know later that it was the Sheesh Mahal in the Lahore Fort. Another thing which clung to her memory was the underground tunnel in the fort which was supposed to open in another city hundreds of miles away. They had quietly descended to one of those secret passages without the help of the guide. It was as dark as night in there. Her father had burned his handkerchief with the cigarette lighter to show them the mouth of the tunnel. She felt as if she were going through that dark passage now. She had no idea where it was going to lead her.

She wanted to concentrate on the future, but her past memories were dragging her back. Was she going too fast into the future? She had read somewhere that if you went close to the speed of light you would be able to see the things behind you.

John wanted to have lunch in a sidewalk restaurant but Qudsia was too terrified to get out and take the risk of being seen by someone. So John bought some food and they ate it by the bank of the canal. The breeze sweeping the water and the green fields around made her drowsy. She slept most of the way to Montgomery.

She suddenly woke up, feeling very hot. She knew instantly that they were crossing the desert near Multan. The sky was hot and the sand-dunes were glistening in the sun. The shadows of the sparse palm trees were lolling like tired animals on the sandy waves. The spiky bushes were looking towards the sky as if begging the heavens for showers. She saw a few caravans of nomads going from one small oasis to another where they would find a mossy pond, the shelter of a few palm trees sprouting from the same root like a finely assorted bouquet, and a patch of grass for their animals to graze on.

How happy and content the people looked sitting on camel-back. They had their families, belongings, cattle and wealth with them. The camels walked in long, leisurely strides, the bells strung to the ribbons around their necks ringing pleasantly, echoing in the desolate desert. Why couldn't she go with the nomads and stay with them for the rest of her life? They looked so free, uninhibited, happy. She would tell them she wanted only freedom and anonymity. Wouldn't they accept her? She knew in her heart that it was as hard for them to accept her in their way of life as it would have been for her to welcome them into her parents' set-up. She would be a misfit there as she was in Shahzore's house.

The evening sun on the horizon started sinking rapidly. There were red, orange, purple and grey streaks in the sky. As it set, these stripes of colour gradually mixed with increasing darkness. Soon it was totally dark and a new scare started to sprout in her heart. She still lay on the back seat. Sometimes the approaching light of a car would throw its beam on them and then it would all be dark again.

It was almost midnight when she felt that the car had changed its route and advanced on a narrow dirt road. After about a quarter of an hour it came to a halt. Qudsia sat up in her seat and cautiously looked out. She saw a building of moderate size surrounded by trees with an outbuilding at a short distance.

John got out, stretched himself like a tired lion and went towards the outhouse. Soon he came back with the caretaker of the rest house, giving him instructions to fix something to eat. He did not throw a hint that there was another person with him. When the man offered to take the bags into the rest house, John said, 'No, there is no need to take them in as I will leave very early tomorrow morning. Please do something about the food. If nothing is available, an omelette will do. Then make the bed and go home. Don't worry about the dishes. I'll put them in the kitchen and you can wash them in the morning.'

Qudsia heard the whole conversation and noticed that John acted as if he were alone. She knew that he was cautious, but his asking for a meal for one person and making one bed made her very uncomfortable. John went in with the humble dinner of omelette and bread to the bedroom and put it on the table between the two armchairs.

'Come on, Qudsia, let's eat. I want to go to sleep as soon as possible. I'm dead tired. Today I can sleep on a scaffold, as the Urdu saying goes.'

Qudsia went into the bathroom, washed her hands and face and joined him for dinner; but she hardly ate a thing. After dinner John carried the dishes to the kitchen and came back.

'Listen Qudsia,' he said, 'I know you're scared to death, but don't be afraid of me. Have faith in me and everything is going to be all right.' Then he smiled and added, 'Maybe we have forcefully occupied countries and established colonies, but we respect women. I, at least, would consider it beneath my dignity to have a woman without her consent. I'm not going to bother you in any way. Just lock the door and go to sleep. I have locked all the doors from inside.' He smiled to reassure her. 'There are other rooms in the building and plenty of bedding, so don't worry about me. I'll knock at your door early in the morning half an hour before leaving. Be ready, and we will leave quietly. This will be the last leg of our journey. Once we reach Karachi, we'll be safe.'

'I hope so,' Qudsia said softly.

'Let's hope for the best. Good night.'

He closed the door behind him and Qudsia secured it at once. Then she went to the window and looked out. It was a moonlit night; very still, not even a leaf was moving. The continuous sound of flowing river had become a part of the silent night. Suddenly she felt a strange courage and strength coming to her from nowhere; everything had gone fine so far. Soon they would be out of danger and she would be able to decide what she wanted to do with her life. She was not sleepy at all. She wanted to feel her newly gained freedom all by herself. After all, she had no one but herself to live her life. John was a liberator, a person who had opened the door of the cage and he would stay so as far as she was concerned. Now it would depend on the strength of her own wings to assure her how far and how long she could fly! Feeling happy and confident for the first time since she had left her house, she opened the door, slid into the hall and sneaked out of the rest house. There was a path, half hidden with bushes and shrubberies. Taking that path she reached the bank of the river. There she sat on the cool, wet sand like a happy and contented child. It was such a forsaken place! The caretaker of the house must be the only living soul here for miles, she thought, and he would never come out of his house at this late hour. She was completely free to enjoy the moonlit night and her solitude.

She sat there bathed in perfect calm and beauty for a few minutes. Suddenly she heard a rustle of clothes and footsteps on the sand approaching her. She had her back to that side, so she did not know who it was. Her blood froze in her veins and she held her breath in the faint hope that it was only her imagination. Then she saw a long shadow falling in front of her and heard John's voice: 'Is that you, Qudsia?'

He advanced slowly and, coming close, sat beside her. 'Are you feeling any better?' he asked.

'Much better,' she answered. 'This is the first time I have started to feel free. I even managed to come out of the house as I was sure there wouldn't be anyone out here at this hour. This is great, isn't it?'

'Yes, it is, and it's going to be better still. Qudsia, I believe that everybody has a right to be free. Nobody can keep you chained like an animal. You are now out of reach of your husband and in-laws and can demand justice. The law would be on your side, I know that.'

He kept on talking, encouraging her in one way or the other while she was thinking all the time, 'Has this all been happening in a dream?' It could not be real for her to be sitting on the bank of a river at night and with a stranger, too!

'What are you thinking about?' John countered. He bent towards her as if to tell her a secret. 'Listen to me. A piece of rock can remain hidden in a drain or in a corner of a street, but do you think a diamond can remain hidden from the eyes of folks?' He smiled and his eyes glistened in the last rays of the setting moon.

The truth of what he had just said started sinking in. She was a pretty, young, educated woman. She might remain obscure in a Western five-star hotel but not in the average district of Karachi.

A renewed feeling of helplessness gripped her. John was unaware of that. As she was drawing some figures on the sand, he started philosophizing. 'As a matter of fact, today's man can never get himself lost, either in the Black Forest of Germany or in the green jungles of Africa. Every bit of land is owned by somebody. They ask questions: "Where do you come from?" "Where are you going?" Then there are passports and visas to let you into a country for only a certain amount of time. I tell you, Qudsia, the golden age of *Ramayana* when people could go and live wherever they wanted is left far behind. Do you know that? There was a time I felt exactly the same, that one day I would get down from a bus in an obscure place in some part of the world and just get myself lost. It's not possible.'

He paused and then continued, 'Let me suggest something. You go to England and complete your studies. I know you will be happy there. You could wear Western dress and speak English and no one would know you are not English.' He smiled encouragingly again.

Before Qudsia could reply, she heard a faint noise behind her.

Then she felt a powerful hand on her shoulder and on her mouth and a heavy sack over her head. She lost all consciousness.

The darkness of that moment when the cloth was thrown over her head and she was carried like a bag on a shoulder turned out to be her fate for ever. She was never again allowed to leave the house. In the beginning she kept waiting to be poisoned or shot, but nothing happened except that one night her husband came to her.

'Tell me the truth,' he said. 'Did that foreigner sleep with you?'

Qudsia was aghast. She did not know how to phrase her answer. After a moment she decided to say it as John had put it. 'They may look very immoral to you, but they think it below their dignity to have a woman without her consent.'

She saw her husband's colour change. In extreme rage he shouted like a madman. 'All right, from now on I will never take a woman without her consent.' Then he closed the door behind him and never came back, not for thirty years. She came to know later through Gulshan *Dai* that her life was spared only because she was pregnant before she left. She had heard her mother-in-law saying to her son, 'By killing her, you would kill your child too! It may be a boy, who knows!'

After his son was born, she waited for her death afresh, but the fatal moment had probably passed. She was now shown her son, but her husband never came to see her again. Soon after the birth, all the furniture given by her father was taken out of her room and was replaced by a few very old pieces. To her great anguish, the bookcase with all the books was taken to the guest room. She was still the junior Khan's wife, but in name only.

Aijaz closed the diary and started packing. Soon afterwards, Nasir came and explained to him that they would be taking two different routes and would meet at a certain point. Nasir would take his mother while Aijaz would go with a confidant. At the secret rendezvous, they would have a car ready, by which they would travel further together. Nasir left in haste and Aijaz accompanied the confidant. They went stealthily to the back of the house, rode the horses and descended the narrow path between the hills. It was a dark night but the horses seemed to know the way. Aijaz was having mixed feelings: the fear of being caught and the thrill of adventure. He couldn't entertain those ambivalent emotions for long, as the man accompanying him came closer, grabbed him and put something over his nose. Aijaz blacked out.

When Aijaz regained his senses, he found himself lying on the back seat of a cab. How he came to be there he had no idea. It was a bright, sunny day and the rays of the sun were falling directly on his eyes. He started to recollect the events of the night before.

'Where are you taking me?' he asked the driver. A hefty man sitting beside the driver looked back and said something in his own dialect, not to Aijaz but to the driver. The driver pulled up by the side of the road. The man on the front seat got out and came over to Aijaz.

'Here's your wallet,' he said, giving the wallet to Aijaz. 'Count your money and check other things. Your suitcase is in the trunk of the car. The elder Khan wants you to take the taxi as far as Rawalpindi; after that you will be on your own. Take a train and go straight to Karachi. Don't say a word to anybody about the incident and never try to come back to the village. Do you understand?'

'Yes, but where is Nasir Khan?' asked Aijaz.

'I was instructed to tell you this much only,' the man said sternly and moved up to the driver.

'You can continue,' he said. 'I will take a bus from here and go back.'

Evidently he had his orders from the elder Khan, and so did the taxi driver, because he did not answer any of the questions Aijaz put to him.

'Where shall I drop you?' asked the driver.

'Wherever you like,' Aijaz said angrily. 'May the devil take you,' he mumbled grudgingly.

'Then there's no need for me to go to Rawalpindi, you can as well take the train from Nowshera,' said the driver.

'That's fine with me,' Aijaz said indignantly.

They did not talk to each other after that. Aijaz was drowned in his nightmarish thoughts. The happenings of the last few days were like a dream, absolutely unbelievable. God only knew what had happened to Nasir and his mother. Was it possible that they had escaped from the clutches of the elder Khan? It was highly unlikely, but what the elder Khan was going to do with them was something Aijaz could not think of.

The driver stopped his taxi in the main bazaar of the small town of Nowshera. Unceremoniously, he took out the suitcase from the car, dropped it on the sidewalk and left without a word. Aijaz felt humiliated but there was nothing he could do about it.

He didn't have to wait long. Within half an hour, he saw an approaching bus with a sign reading Rawalpindi. He jumped in with his suitcase. Buying a ticket, he seated himself comfortably. The whole episode of the previous night became vague and misty, as if it had all happened long, long ago.

Once in Karachi, Aijaz waited for Nasir Khan or a word from him, but neither came. Then he wrote letters to Nasir but never received an answer. He still had Nasir Khan's belongings in his possession and often thought about him.

For the next three years he kept himself busy with his residency, then secured a nice job in a reputable hospital and finally got married. They chose the beautiful valley of Swat for their honeymoon. Since Nasir's village was not far from there, Aijaz decided to go there as well. He narrated the whole story to his wife and, with her consent, went to see Nasir alone. Everything was as enchantingly beautiful there as ever. He started climbing the steep path to the house. As he approached, he could see the hanging terrace suspended in the air. He saw the elder Khan sitting there on the wooden *takht*, reclining on a huge round pillow, just like the olden days. Aijaz advanced a little, then realized that it was none other than Nasir Khan. Aijaz hastily came out of the cover and rushed towards him. Nasir Khan did not immediately recognize him but when he did, he jumped towards Aijaz and took him in a friendly embrace. Nasir Khan forthwith postponed the meeting he was holding and sent away his servants on various errands so that he could be alone with Aijaz.

'Why didn't you come to Karachi?' Aijaz asked impatiently as soon as they were alone. 'And why, for God's sake, didn't you write to me?'

'Be patient, my friend,' Nasir Khan smiled pleasantly. 'It's a long story. You don't expect me to tell you in one sentence, do you?'

'Of course not, but tell me what happened! Do you know that I had to reconcile myself to the idea that you were no longer alive?'

Nasir Khan laughed heartily. 'Don't be ridiculous! We Khans love our children more than anything in the world, especially our sons. We cannot harm them in any way. I told you it's a long story. I shall tell you after meals when we have our siesta and nobody is likely to disturb us.'

'No, I cannot wait. I'm dying to know why I was so dramatically sent away from here and never heard from you after that.'

'OK, take a seat, make yourself comfortable,' said Nasir Khan. 'I'm going to tell you everything right away.'

Aijaz sat on a chair nearest the settee, facing the river, and looked at Nasir expectantly.

'As you left us,' said Nasir Khan, 'I went to get Mother. She asked me to come in, but behaved very strangely. She hugged and kissed me and asked to stay for one more day. I told her that you had already left and that it would create a lot of trouble for you, but she insisted that I wait for one more day. At last I gave in, thinking that you would manage somehow.

'After I came back to my room, Gulshan *Dai* knocked at my door and gave me a short note. It was from my mother, saying, "I don't see any point in going with you. It would be disastrous for both of us. I want you to believe that your mother died at the time when you were born. That's all. Goodbye, my dearest."'

Nasir took a deep breath, glanced at the river and said, 'My mother was sure that if she went with me, my father would disinherit me from the estate and everything else. Not knowing what to do, she decided to commit suicide. Perhaps she had been putting it off for years till such time that she could see me. She went to the cliff to plunge into the river and end her life. She was caught because she was still being watched against leaving the house any time of the day or night.

'That night was the night when she met her husband after thirty years. Just visualize the scene: it was this very place. The moon had come up late that night, as you know already. The marble bench made me feel as if it were a dream. My mother, stately, dignified and still glamorous as a goddess, came walking slowly as she had been told to do. My father saw her and winced. She might have been as delicate as a water lily in her youth, but she looked like a marble statue now, lifeless, but larger than life. Elder Khan's heart softened. He went to her with great poise and confidence.

'"Qudsia, I pardon you today," he said in a soft but still an authoritative tone. "God be my witness."

'Mother remained silent for a moment, then she looked up. Their eyes met. "I want to make a confession," she said in a firm voice. "I had lied to you before. The foreigner did . . . touch . . . me but not without my consent." After saying this, she, with measured steps, disappeared into the female quarters.

'She refused to see anybody and was never seen again by others. She even stopped giving orders to the servants and refused to talk.

'My father, a tyrant, soon became a pathetic figure. He wanted to see her so that she could once say that what she told him that night was a lie; but she declined to see him. He even begged me to go and plead for him, but Mother stood like a rock. Father died shortly after, but Mother never saw him till the last day.'

Nasir was silent for a few moments, then he spoke again. 'I want to ask you a question. Do you believe the statement she made before my father was correct? What do you think?'

'I think it was totally incorrect,' Aijaz said emphatically. 'Didn't she tell you that she had written a true account in her diary?'

'I know, but why did she have to say what she did to my father?'

'She said it to shatter his ego. She was punished heavily for something she had not done. It was her way of taking revenge.'

'Yes, you're right, and she did.'

As Nasir said those words, Aijaz saw a beautiful young woman coming towards them from the house. She was dressed in modern clothes and by her looks seemed an educated city woman – quite an alien to that part of the country.

Nasir saw her too. He smiled and said, 'Come, dear, meet my buddy Aijaz whom I have been talking about so much.'

'Aijaz, this is my wife Naeema,' said Nasir, introducing her.

Aijaz stood up to pay his respects. After chatting for a short while, she left.

After she was gone, Nasir said, 'I have done away with the old customs. We don't have separate suites for men and women any more. I take my wife everywhere with me. I took her down to the river the very second day of my marriage, and I could see how happy my mother was for both of us.' Nasir bent towards Aijaz as if to tell him a secret.

'I make it a point to introduce Naeema to a foreigner if one comes to visit our place. I don't know why I do it,' Nasir said.

Aijaz smiled because he knew perfectly well why he did that.

English version by the author

Fahmida Riaz

Some Misaddressed Letters

1

When 'B' was murdered in a bleak cell of Kot Lakhpat gaol in Pakistan, Amina was in Delhi. Someone had knocked at the door of her hotel room in the morning. Amina opened the door. It was one of the host poets. He did not come inside. He looked pale, almost guilty.

'What is it?' asked Amina, not at all thinking about 'B'. She thought the poetry recital had been cancelled.

'They've hanged him,' he said quietly, avoiding her eyes. They had dragged the case against 'B' so long that the Indians had become deeply involved.

Amina felt numb and cold.

'When?'

'This morning, at 4 o'clock.'

Numbness again. Many thoughts flitted through her mind. Then she said, listening carefully to her own words, 'I always knew. I told Murad so many times. But Murad wouldn't believe I always knew. Murad is so hopelessly over-optimistic. Naive, that's what he is.'

As she finished her querulous flat outburst, she was already taking decisions. Various statements of politicians and the intelligentsia that she had collected to save 'B' were now useless. Better tear them up right here. But the books? How to smuggle them to Karachi? Earlier, a friend in the airlines had promised to quietly carry the packets. Now he may not. She must meet him and retrieve them. She must keep her appointment in the Pakistan embassy. In the evening there was a *mushaira* at the ambassador's residence. She must go there as well. Act normal.

In the Pakistan embassy there was a diplomat who had had the queerest relations with Amina. One important part of it was that during the course of the fifteen years that they had known each other, the two letters Amina had sent him had come back to her stamped all over, 'Address incorrect'. They had wandered from place to place, from one desk to another, and finally, not finding the addressee anywhere, were sent back to her by the post office. Between the sending of the two letters there was a space of several years. They were sent to two different countries. This was a strange coincidence and Amina often wondered if providence had something to do with the twice-repeated non-delivery.

But Amina was truly fond of this friend of hers. Their friendship of mistaken addresses was long, untarnished, undemanding and gentle.

Long ago, when she was still in college and he had just joined the Department of Foreign Services, they had met and instantly liked each other. Amina had fallen in love with him but he had gently discouraged her. However, young aspiring poets in India are by literary tradition trained not to register the clearest message of rejection. Indeed, some of the best poetry sings of such unilateral passions. It is a poetry of savouring one's own longing and the many wondrous ways in which it manifests itself. In the Indian classics, this love is like the stilled flame of the candle upon which the yogi and the sufi fix their gaze. (In other cultures this one-sided perseverance may appear entirely useless and laughable!)

For Amina, her love for this young man was like the legendary flame in the faraway palace on which the washerman fixed his gaze as he stood in the freezing waters of the Yamuna through a long, cold night. You do not notice when the first lights of dawn gently unveil the sky and the flame melts into daylight, imperceptibly bringing into relief the sprawling landscape, the vision of the palace itself on the distant banks of the Yamuna.

'What prize? No prize?' says the king the next day. 'This man achieved no feat. He was warmed by the candle flame in our palace.'

But the wise minister tells the king, 'The candle flame gave him no warmth. He was sustained by his own gaze.'

The king stood corrected. The washerman was given the prize. Amina too walked out of her watershed with her first volume of poems. Its publication and that it was well-received had decisively set the course of her life.

Now the letters. They were not love letters. They were written to him during the Indo-Pakistan war of 1965. The second one was written to him immediately before the Indo-Pakistan war of 1971, when the Pakistan army was massacring Bengalis. Why in the world were they written to him who had never shown her the slightest interest in things political? Books, music, paintings were what they mostly talked about. Once when she told him on the phone she was reading history, he had said with regret, 'Don't waste your time.'

He believed in the eternal separation of the 'world outside' and his inner life. The flow of his inner life was undoubtedly beautiful, reflecting images of a very delicate beauty, much like a Chinese painting. And Amina . . . She was forever shooting off tangents into the 'outside'. Should we have a war with India? Should the Bengalis be massacred in our name?

Twice she had tried to make contact and misaddressed her letters. Now as she walked towards his room, she was vaguely curious.

2

He was standing by his table to receive her. Suddenly she was very happy to see him, his familiar face, the same moronic smile.

They wondered about the coincidence that they had met again, without ever making the smallest effort. When she was in London, he was posted there and now in Delhi, of all places.

They talked of Urdu poetry in India.

'Are you coming to the *mushaira* tonight at the ambassador's house?' she asked.

He looked disconcerted. Now there was no escaping the question. Nabbed at last, thought Amina.

Then he said in his deliberate stammer, half-sentences, measured usually to communicate the depth of his feelings, the turbulence of his mind, 'I'm not coming. I don't know.' Pause. 'I feel like someone . . .', pause, 'who is there to look after something', pause, 'and', pause, 'it is not being looked after very well.'

Amina was beginning to feel exhausted. She looked at the room, the flowers, the photograph of the Founding Father on the wall. She knew how he felt, knew that despite his affected mannerisms, he was really feeling sick at heart. But there was a difference. The root of his anguish lay in his own choice. He was not frightened like Amina. She smiled sweetly and bade him goodbye. She had just seen the face of rampant angst.

On her way back in the taxi she murmured to herself, 'Brother, now that was some misaddressed meeting!'

3

Ever since she had sought asylum in India, Amina had patiently resigned herself to the new reality that in her host country, every communal riot, every major derailment, every electricity failure was now her personal responsibility. This was not merely symptomatic of burgeoning megalomania; she was suffering the ultimate fate of all political refugees, insomuch as she too had fallen prey to the curse of averted disaster, the maledictions of deferred imprisonment and thwarted interrogations. Political refugees all over the world suffer this malady as they shoulder the burden of all the sins of the host country. It is no use trying to reason with oneself that, after all, refuge was sought to avoid personal persecution, imprisonment, perhaps even physical torture during interrogation and this act is in no way a declaration to the world that the host country is a virtual paradise on earth. Self-righteous postures cannot assuage his suffering. It only adds to his guilt, the humiliation of a defensive argument.

In the host country no one looks down on the political refugee. People sympathize with him and bring him baskets of fruit and bouquets. He will now live like a chronic invalid. One can really enjoy it for a while. But the question is, what would one say? Hospitality is only confounding his predicament further. He knows he is in a position where he can neither be natural nor honest. Because for the political refugee, the honest thing to do is really to write odes in praise of the host country which would embarrass all concerned beyond recourse and make him look like a perfect ass.

Then what is he to do? He feels (a little bird tells him) that his only chance of redemption lies in picking faults with the host country; only that would be the irrefutable proof of his still intact integrity. He would thus show the world that he is still his old critical self. More often than not, the ploy works beautifully. It saves his position in the eyes of the people, and that, God knows, is more than half the story of all our lives.

Amina wrote a number of passionate poems, exposing the gaping flaws in a democratic system that still allowed for horrifying poverty. She read them to a select gathering of Indian writers. The Indian intelligentsia, which has rarely known persecution since the last half-century, which is free to choose between the right and the left, between east and west, or north and south, is always thrilled by chastisement. They warmly smiled at her. One of them remarked, 'It is a very sincere attempt.'

These words at once revealed to Amina that she had just posted another misaddressed letter.

It takes some time, but you come to know that when you are saying all the right things for the wrong reasons, you are only playing to the gallery of your own doubts and misgivings.

Amina's misaddressed letters had tried to tell her just that.

4

Months passed into years before they would buy crockery in Delhi. Buying anything here appeared to them as a gross waste of money since it was to be left behind when they went back.

When the last teacup given them as a gift by friends got broken by accident, they had no choice but to buy a tea set.

When they went to buy the tea set, it became acutely clear to Murad that they had still not gone back. No one around them could understand why purchasing cups was causing such anguish to this couple in exile.

Instead of the usual six cups that came with a tea set, Murad bought twelve cups. He convinced Amina that it was essential to buy extra cups so that if one cup was broken, the tea set might not look incomplete. But the real reason for his buying extra cups was that he never wanted to enter the shop again.

When a friend presented them with a packet of seeds, Murad was both amused and irritated. He felt that it was extraordinarily presumptuous of their friend to present them with something that needed time to grow and might bear flowers.

He hid the packet away in a drawer of the kitchen table.If they were to remain there for those months, during which the seedlings could sprout and grow and bear flowers, what could they do with the flower pots when they went back? They could not possibly carry flower pots to another country. They would have to be left behind or just given away. Both of them had become averse to the idea of leaving things behind.

The aversion was obviously rooted in their abandoning all their possessions when they escaped from their country with roughly scribbled notes to relatives instructing them to dispose of their belongings as best they could.

After some years, there was an uprising in their country. Murad kept his calm and spoke dispassionately to their friends about the expected success or failure of the uprising. It was during those days that he purchased some flower pots. He found the forgotten packet of seeds in one of the drawers of the kitchen board and planted them, assiduously. He took a long time filling every pot with earth, planting the seed and mixing fertilizer with earth to fill the flower pot. When all the seeds were planted, he placed them in a neat row. All he could do next was to go round them seven times (which he did not) to wind up the ritual.

The ritual of seed planting was unintentionally devised by Murad to ward off the evil of hope.

5

Ever since they had set foot in their country of exile, Murad had hated nothing more than hope, no matter how he vexed eloquent in its praise. Hope always filled him with such shame that he regretted ever getting himself in a situation where hope and hopelessness became indispensable parts of everyday life. He was convinced that if hope left him alone, his life could be far better.

In normal conditions, hope, the shame and curse of all mortals, remained reasonably diffused, spreading itself thinly on such objectives as catching a bus or obtaining an advertisement for their journal. But now all hope converged on a single point, straining for the overthrow of the military regime in their country. Consequently if he missed a bus, it irritated him to no end because he had ceased to even consider the possibility that a bus could be missed, and therefore when he left his house for the bus stop, he never hoped to catch the bus but rather hoped to buy the newspaper.

Murad needed no one to tell him that to hope was the worst possible state to be in. The opposite of hope is despair, to which he never gave a thought, perhaps because his soul had always known it. But it is wrongly assumed that a despairing soul knows no hope, which again torments only the despairing soul. An incurable optimist is never tormented by hope. For him, failure is a plaything, a magic ball that he throws up in the air with a silent 'hurrah!' and no matter where it falls, it is again in his hands because it is a magic ball, and he is ready to throw it up once more, himself always lightly floating several feet above ground.

Murad had never failed in achieving his objectives so that he knew nothing about failure. He began his life in utter poverty where hope flapped its wings and circled overhead like vultures above the marshland by the river where carcasses of dead animals lay rotting.

Murad's hatred for hope was similar to his hatred for Amina.

How to be rid of hope: that was the question. It was not naivety but need that gave rise to hope. He thought that it would be best if he changed the nature of hope. One never hopes for the best (what a lark that is). One always hopes only for just a little. But Murad set his heart on hoping for the worst (that still did not stop him from secretly preparing for something that should be a little better than the worst).

But the secret preparations were in vain. The uprising was crushed. A village was bombarded. Nearly one thousand people died. Many more thousands were imprisoned.

Murad went on a spree of purchasing flower pots and planting seedlings. Meantime the first-sown seeds were already sprouting. In a matter of months, their tiny flat was full of plants. He had grown too attached to them so that the very thought of leaving them behind or giving them away would break his heart. Murad looked at his plants as his secret battlefield to combat hope. Yet it was only one morning as he was hoeing the pots, picking out earth worms, that he had thought, if one uprising is crushed, can another be far behind?

6

The word 'uprising' always reminded Murad of a minuscule uprising in a village that did not fail and another uprising in his own body that did.

In Colarchi, a small village in Pakistan, the landowner was not only rich but also a local intellectual. He was a pal of the local assistant commissioner and their evenings were spent drinking whisky and reciting poetry to each other. The assistant commissioner was grateful to him for both, because where else in that God-forsaken village could he find whisky and poetry at the same time and in the same place?

As a direct result of this friendship, the landowner was convinced that if the *haris*, the peasants, demanded half the crop (as they were legally entitled) he would have no difficulty in getting them all locked up in a jiffy. The *haris* were demanding the full half-crop. The landlord threatened to sack them all and eject them and their families from his lands. As the crops ripened for harvest, the dispute remained unresolved.

When the harvesting was done, the landlord went to the assistant commissioner. '"B" has turned their heads,' said the landlord. 'He tells us one thing and tells them another. To us he says, "*Yaar*, I'm only talking." To them he says, "Go, go, get the full half-crop." Let us call their bluff. Lock them up.'

The *haris* were arrested and sent to the lock-up.

It so happened that Colarchi was a stronghold of Murad's revolutionary group. (Here 'stronghold' means the strength of seven peasants or less.) One of their comrades came rushing to the cell. The cell rushed back to the village and asked the womenfolk to guard the harvest.

The landowner had hired local bandits to carry the harvest to his personal *godown*. The peasants would have been reduced to a mushy pulp, oozing red liquid, by these bandits, because they were truly ferocious. But when the bandits reached Dera and saw women guarding the harvest, they ran back as fast as if they had seen the very demons of hell.

Their loose pants of nine yards flapping in the wind, they folded their hands: 'Raise a hand against other people's women! No, *Baba*, no! This cannot be,' said the bandits.

The landowner had overlooked what one of the bandits was now telling him in no uncertain words: 'We may be bandits, but we are not, what you call . . . buggers. We have our own mothers, sisters, daughters. In every trade there is a code of conduct. What if someone attacks our women while we are away? What would happen to our banditry then?'

Getting the peasants arrested was a mistake.

Meanwhile, a camel caravan was proceeding under the bright starry sky, softly tinkling its bells, on the soft, cool sandy dunes of Colarchi. It carried the full half-crop to the next village (where the cell was located), and before dawn was distributed among the peasants' mothers, sisters, daughters.

7

The second uprising occurred when behind the huge haystack, under that bright starry sky, the *hariani* smiled. When she smiled she lowered her gaze. The next moment, all Murad could see superimposed on the lowered gaze was the photograph of her husband, the group leader! The Comrade! And he couldn't do it. Not for his life. He could not cuckold the Comrade now panting and running on the sandy dunes with the camels. Half of the mind says, fool, if you don't . . . someone else will. But it fails to rise. What rises in its place is a huge admonishing finger and a booming voice that says, your brother's honour, etc. The voice of his father, or grandfather or great-grandfather, or all of them rolled into one. Fraternity seeps into the legs and melts the kneecaps. Camaraderie asserts itself through impotence! The *hariani* smiles with contempt. An unforgettable smile . . .

English version by the author

Jamila Hashmi

Exile

Sita of the Indian epic the Ramayana *followed her husband Rama into exile, then was abducted by the demon-king Ravana in whose kingdom she chose exile in a grove rather than marrying him and enjoying the privileges of being queen. When Rama eventually rescued her and brought her back to his kingdom, she was forced into exile because the people of their kingdom impugned her chastity as she had lived away so long.* (Translator's note)

The birds fly, beating their wings faster and faster and the sun has turned yellow and descended to the steps of the large lake of Uchal. The setting rays turn the colour of the *gurdvara* spikes a gold-tinged white. And on the other side of the large common, the Dusehra fair is beginning to disperse. Now, in a little while, the effigies of the demon Ravana will be set alight. People will create a clamour as they run about, afraid, and in the blue twilight the embers will look like descending sparklers. The flames will rise for a long time and the faces of the people round about will look fearsome in the firelight, as if each one is a disguised Ravana seeking Sita to gloat over her isolation and her second exile.

Exile is such a hard thing. But nothing is in anyone's power. Who accepts suffering from choice? *Bhai* used to say, 'Bibi, why are you always dreaming? This love that you enjoy, this gaiety all around you, they will slowly lessen. Time reduces everything. But the deterioration comes so slowly that we get used to it.' Where is my brother today? This breeze that travels with me, carrying the smell of my birthplace, if it knew where he was too, I'd tell it, 'Ask him, will you, why this pain won't lessen? Even after hauling their burden for years across arduous paths, why do people still dream? Why do they yearn for peace and why do they love the light?'

Why was Sita's only prayer in exile to be reunited with Ramchandra? Doesn't misfortune harden people enough to abandon the hope of good times? After all, why can't we love darkness? Why?

The *naak* tree has been flowering since the year Munni was born. The seasons change and its branches are smothered in blossom and the tree bows with the weight of its flowers. The union of the tree and the soil grows deeper. Its roots stretch further into the ground – no one can sever that relationship.

Munni has grown up now. How soundlessly the footsteps of time have passed me by. Today *Bari Ma* said to Gurpal, '*Kaka*, take my *bahu* and the children to the Dusehra fair. She hasn't left the village for years.'

Gurpal said sharply, 'Mother, when did you ever ask me to take them? It's not my fault she hasn't been anywhere for years.'

Who can be to blame? When someone calls me *bahu*, daughter-in-law, I feel they're abusing me. I've been hearing it for years. Since that night when Gurpal jostled me into the courtyard and spoke to *Bari Ma* as she sat on her stool.

'Look, Mother, I've brought you a *bahu*. Winsome and pretty. She's the best of today's haul.' And Ma approached me, raising the lamp flame. My eyes protruded from hunger and fear. The barefoot trudge, miles long, had left me without the strength to raise a finger. I slumped in a heap at her feet. The cow and buffaloes tethered in the courtyard abandoned their fodder and stood staring at me. *Bari Ma* looked me up and down several times and said, 'If Gurpal did a decent day's work, I wouldn't be in this state today. Look at me, I'm almost blind from fanning the fire. And all the maids have stopped calling because our harvest wasn't in on time. Tell me how I'm supposed to handle the burden of this house. If only you'd start farming – I'd be so delighted.'

Gurpal said, 'But look. You won't have to put up with the airs and graces of casual labour any more. You've got your own serving girl now. Set her to the grindstone, make her draw the water – whatever you like. I'm not obligated to her. I've brought you a *bahu*.'

All Sangrao was filled with *bahus*. But no one sang wedding songs to the beat of drums. Nor did the dancing-girls make bawdy jokes or swing their hips and make fun. No one oiled my dust-stiffened hair, nor did any matron groom me. I became a bride but my hands were not decorated with henna, nor was my parting dressed with bridal red. No palanquin came to take me away.

Bari Ma listened to Gurpal, looking at me as if I was a burden that her grandson had picked up somewhere. Then she went inside again with the lamp and no one bothered about me. What a welcome for a *bahu*!

From that day to this, I'm Sita. I'm enduring exile and I'm a prisoner in Sangrao. Uprooting their swings and swigging *bidis*, the swing-men are mucking about with each other. They dump their wares so roughly on the donkeys, you'd think the animals were made of wood. The bullock carts of the Ram-Leela performers are standing to one side and the acting-boys eat creamy *kulfi* and *pakoras* with chutney, unmindful of their shiny clothes. The stains look like dung marks on their colourful clothes. Munni stands gaping at them. She doesn't realize she could get lost. What difference does awareness make? If someone's to be lost, they can disappear from a full house.

Gurpal is tugging her; and both the boys, tired, crying, demand something from every vendor they see. Is this a fair?

Mothers are pushed around in the crowd, nonchalant about their children, and get detached from them. Small children, staring into each face, cry loudly and walk on. Tell me, do people separated in fairgrounds ever meet again? The separation becomes a barrier between the generations. Our eyes are never graced with the faces we long to see just once more. Our paths close up behind us like patterns on the weft and woof of cloth. We cannot retrace our footsteps on the road we have walked. Nothing comes back. And the crowd at the fair moves forward, always forward.

Time never returns. *Bhai* used to say, '*Bibi*, the moment that's passed is erased. It turns to dust.' I wouldn't pay attention, getting engrossed, instead, in playing with my doll's house with my friends as soon as I came back from school. *Bhaiyya* tried to counsel me.

My father had bought me that doll's house. He'd bought it from an exhibition. Munni tenderly clutches a largish cloth doll. Gurpal watches the crowd above. And Munni bends again and again to look at her doll. Both the boys are carrying idols of Ravana and gaping at every passing face with astonished expressions. Munni's eyes hold so much love for her doll. Its nose and eyes are defined in crude stitches on its wide cloth face. There's a ring in its nose. Its gold-edged mantle is tacked to her head as she clutches her long skirt. It makes her look like a dancing-girl. Now she'll dance. Our route to Sangrao runs past the shores of Lake Uchal. Life's caravan moves on, through twisted paths and straight ones, and tangled foot tracks, even if we reach our goal along the way – we must keep walking. For ever, for ever, even if our feet are wounded and there's nothing in our hearts.

The blue dusk descends further. I don't know why, the evenings make me indescribably unhappy. One star is leaping, throbbing, shuddering like the wick of a lamp in its blue, empty sea; its isolation reminds me of my exile. In my isolation, I'm like a lone tree which neither fruits nor flowers. This star reminds me of the ship on which *Bhai* went to sea. As he prepared to go abroad, surrounded with piles of baggage, *Amma*'s voice was drenched in tears but she packed calmly for him and prayed. Outside *Baba* was involved in all kinds of arrangements and *Bhaiyya* was despondent. *Apa* paced up and down the inner courtyard with silent footsteps. I pranced around the house, chirping – who feels the severity of pain before being wounded?

We had all gone to see him off at the harbour. *Bhaiyya* went off to sort out the paperwork for *Bhai*'s luggage. I bent over the rail watching the brackish water and asked *Bhai*, 'Why is this water like this? Why is it oil-stained? Why do they have lifeboats here? What is the paddle for? Why the anchor? Doesn't it scare you to see the boats bobbing up and down on the waves?' Pestered by the questions, *Bhai* was saying, 'When you grow up you'll known all the answers automatically, Bibi.'

And today, I do know. The ship that doesn't have an oar, drowns. Boats can even drown at the shoreline. A single wave is enough to drown them. Now that I've grown up and discovered the answers, *Bhai* isn't here any more.

Then the ship's whistles sounded and *Baba* embraced *Bhai* and ran his hand over his head and said, 'Well then, son, I hand you to God.' *Bhaiyya* hugged *Bhai* and soft-hearted *Apa* cried at everything. Seeing her hiccuping sobs, *Bhai* said, 'Look at Bibi, how happy she looks. What's there to cry about? I'll be back in two years. It's not as if I'm leaving for ever.' Then he hugged me to his heart and said, 'Bibi, I'll bring you gifts from Paris. Just keep writing to me.' I nodded vigorously. The last whistle sounded and he walked away, easily, nonchalantly, as if he was just going round the corner. We waved our handkerchiefs as long as we could see the ship, and in the evening haze, the reflected lights of the entire harbour swayed in the water. The light of the ship trembled like a lone star and then vanished. After that, all the lights around me drowned for ever. The waves yielded no light.

How loudly I'd shrieked, clinging to *Amma*. Someone in my heart was saying: You'll never glimpse this face again. You'll never manage to see *Bhai* again. My heart was shuddering like that lone star in the west trembling above the blue dusk in fear.

Far in the gardens, the darkness of night is spreading its wings. Gurpal has hoisted the two boys on his shoulders and they walk ahead of us on footpaths that look like white lines. And Munni walks slowly. By leaping over the ripe crops they will get ahead of us by ten fields, and wait. Gurpal is telling the boys the tale of Ravana. How can he know that I am Sita, following him, and that he himself is Ravana?

Munni says to me, 'Ma, Saroop's uncle gave her some lovely, colourful clothes. They're silk. They're lovely to touch. Ma, don't you have a brother who could send me nice things? Ma, why won't you say anything? You didn't like the fair, did you? Are you tired?'

'Yes, Munni, I'm tired. I've grown old. I've had to walk too far.'

'You're not old at all,' Munni says to me with confidence. 'You're like an icon of the goddess, Ma. *Bari Ma* says so too.'

How should Munni know how much I've had to walk? How great the distance is between one life and another? And when we petrify, there's no hope left in our hearts. That's when we become fit to worship. My eyes have turned to stone, watching, waiting for those separated on the path to Sangrao. My heart is empty. They call me Lakshmi, goddess of fortune, but still the shackles of pain are so unbreakable – profound and strong, they continue to cling.

Munni's asking again, 'Ma, don't you have a brother – a *Mama* for me?' What can I say to her?

How shall I reply? I stand at the fork, reflecting.

I adored *Bhaiyya* but I was quite scared of him. When he entered the house, my *dupatta* seemed to place itself on my head of its own accord, I walked more sedately, I contained my hilarity. When I stood beside him, I felt he was the tallest person in the world. My brother with his careful walk, his gracious speech, his beautiful script. He wrote in straight, clean lines, no scribbles in the margin, no ink-stained hands. He'd say to me, 'Bibi, when you grow up, you'll write like this too.' What would my straight-lined, stainless brother think if he were to see me today? There's so much ink in the scrolls of my destiny that there's not a straight line to be seen on the entire page. I never did learn to write neatly.

In those days, as I arranged the doll's house, I thought we could live in it. *Amma* and *Baba* and I; *Bhaiyya* and *Bhai* and *Apa* too. We'll just live in here. Life is a sweet song, we don't need anything, there's no shortage. When *Bhaiyya* married, I said our home is paradise, a complete and blissful paradise. When I raised my hands to pray in those days, I couldn't think what to ask for. Then, as now, I asked God for nothing. Pain and joy occupy the same point in the circle of life.

Bhai crossed the ocean and my dreams of paradise were shattered. All the pieces of my life have spread here and there, and like glass fragments, their jagged edges wound those who pass. Everyone's feet are wounded, there's no one left to cross to the other side. The road sleeps as if it is passing through a cremation ground. There's no one for miles. Who hears Sita's yearning in that other land? How hard it is, the pain of loneliness – and life. Gurpal is calling me from afar. Calling Munni. We walk slowly. Only sticks remain standing in the cotton fields. People gather up the laughing flowers, take them away. The hairs haven't burst forth yet, nor have the grains formed. Gusts of wind force the tender, flexible plants to bend. You have to bend before the wind. Everyone bends, everyone bows.

Bari Ma must be getting restless. An undefined fear for me forces her heart to pound. The path to the land she's thinking of is tortuous. And after the distance I've walked with Gurpal, I have no strength to walk further. After all, how much can one keep on walking, especially if there's nowhere to go? Where can I take my wounded heart, the unreddened parting in my hair? Munni stands in my way. Munni is a barrier between me and the past. How many distances there are between me and my loved ones. How can I peep beyond her?

The singing-troupes are approaching from behind, singing religious songs. The fair, set up on the shores of Lake Uchal, has disbanded and is strewn into the surrounding pathways. Children cry, men speak in loud voices as they pass Munni and me. Women, wearing their best clothes, holding on to mantles pulled over their foreheads, carry bundles of sweets bought at the fair and clutch their babies at their shoulders, as they walk swiftly by on bare feet. Their shoes, tied in their mantles, swing behind them. There's a deep affinity between soil and feet. Why create a barrier?

As they grow distant, the people become white stains. A yogi turns into the road to Sangrao behind us, strumming his *ektara*. How poignant his voice is. He's right, isn't he, when he says we yearn for light, even knowing it is so insubstantial? I don't hear the melody of his strings, just the occasional word from his song.

'Ma, why are you so quiet? Say something, I'm feeling scared.'

Munni can hardly handle her doll in her attempt to grasp my hand harder. Her voice is drenched in tears. She can't manage another question.

Munni, too, will realize when she grows up that it's useless to fear the dark. When its sorcery begins, it's irresistible. *Bhai* used to say, '*Bibi*, water contains power, it hews its own path.' In those days I couldn't understand his words – where does water get its power? The flow of time hews its own paths. When *Bari Ma* calls to me, I pat the decorative mark into place on my forehead and gently reply, '*Ji*'. I try to dispense with her chores swiftly to keep busy so that I don't have time to think and analyse.

When I had the time I didn't have the perception; now I have that, I have no time. There's always a shortfall and it never goes. This or that always remains incomplete. Today if I shut my eyes, my heart says, 'Your brothers will be here in a moment and as soon as *Bhaiyya* sees me, he'll say, "*Bibi*, what's this disguise? That forehead mark doesn't suit you at all. Remove it. Throw it away. Look what I have for you. Let go of all this. Come here, to me. Sit. Vacations are short and they pass swiftly. Just don't go anywhere when I'm visiting."'

In the large room, we'd sit, looking at pictures, talk, have tea, warm ourselves on the brazier. When we laughed loudly, *Amma* would say in a sleepy voice, 'You've got to get up in the morning. Go to sleep, children.' And *Bhaiyya* would call out louder, '*Amma*, I live away from home all year, sleeping away my misery, what's the hurry? We'll get some sleep eventually, *Amma*.' And I would think, 'These times will turn to dust. The paradise we've created from love will be so obliterated by dust and anonymity that we won't find it again, anywhere.' Like the pictures, we are a reflection of reality. My heart was always crazy, and thought strange, wayward thoughts.

My heart has always indulged in fantasies and throbs pointlessly. When I reason with it, it responds with the question, 'What do you lose, *Bibi*? No one can control fantasy. What's the harm in dreams if they draw in all those whom you await?'

I reply that all I have left are my rights. My heart says it is a sin to lose hope but what shall I hope for?

Munni grabs my mantle and asks, 'Ma, tell me why *Mama* doesn't come here? Can't we go there at Diwali? Ma? All the girls are going. My heart's not in this village any more, Ma. I didn't really enjoy the fair, either. I'm sad. I want to visit my *Mama*'s home.'

Who can I petition for the address of her *Mama*'s house? All the villages outside Sangrao are like doll's houses to me; without a reality; mere shadows of Sangrao. Everything's shadow.

Yet my soul keeps wandering, who knows where, looking for things that were nowhere, longing for voices which I'll never hear again. Why did my heart beat through all the years of heaving baskets on my head, filled with cow dung, milking cows, toasting cow-pats for fuel – every time a sudden scent in the wind brought back the notes of a hundred instruments drawing near? They would carry me far away. Now I know where they all are. And it's a place beyond my reach. Like the road going to Sangrao, all the roads cut across each other as they pass. What's the point of searching for this city of fairy tales?

The tremulous light of lamps, burning inside the open doors of flourishing homes, looks like fairyland. Gurpal and the boys, Munni and I walk together now. The satiny heads on the reeds brush my hair. The wind hugs its satin mantle, slowly drifting into slumber. When I disengage myself from my isolation, the road gets easier.

Munni says, 'Ma, I'm tired, I can't walk any more.' The boys cry and their eyes are drooping with sleep. They can't keep hold of their Ravanas any more and we move off the path onto the low wall of a field. Munni rests her head on my lap. Gurpal is saying, 'Just look how foolish women are. So many children have gone missing today. They lose their heads at the fair and get so involved with the Ram-Leela performances that they let their children drift off.'

'Children are separated from their mothers even without fairs,' I say, stroking Munni's head without looking at him.

'Will you ever be able to forget that incident? Those times were different, it's changed now,' Gurpal says softly.

How can I convince Gurpal that time is never different and people are condemned to suffer because they can't forget? In my memory that scene is alive – fire on all sides, the country had become independent, it had been divided. Father and Mother said, 'All these people are crazy to be flying to another country – can pain touch anyone so close to their dear ones?' *Amma* and *Baba* were so simple – pain always comes from one's near and dear. How real is this worry over which strangers hold sway? Life has lost its beauty and everyone's face is masked in a blast of blood. Those who gave charity in the name of Bhagwan or Allah have run swords across each other's throats. Those who would have died for the honour of their sisters and daughters have forsaken their scruples. The words of brothers and intimates have been cut like the shackles of centuries by independence and partition and ground to dust under the feet of the drifters. *Amma* had told *Baba*, 'We should take the girls and go. I'm frightened – it's useless to trust anyone.'

And *Baba* had said with his usual composure, '*Bibi*'s mother, you're worrying unnecessarily, like everyone else. Tell me, what could go wrong? There had to be a partition. This hue and cry will die down in a few days. Don't worry, all will be well again.' In ordinary circumstances, this answer would have reassured *Amma*, but that day it did not. 'Our lives and honour are both at stake. We have young girls,' she said. 'Listen to me – send me to my brother.'

Baba said, 'The roads are filled with vagabonds who have strayed out of their villages. They're smashing up vehicles. It's more dangerous to go out – better you stay quietly at home. God will protect us.'

Baba must have been worried by the situation but he didn't ask anyone for help except God. *Baba*'s only fault was to have trusted the old values. So it was that when Gurpal dragged me away as the result of that mistake, I saw Father's white head lying by the bank of the canal. His body was in the water. He had somehow found the strength to rise above his closed eyes and bloodied head and pray. Was this the time for prayers to be accepted, you tell me? A shining spear had pierced through *Amma*'s breast and she had fallen where she had prayed to God to protect her life and chastity. *Apa*'s screams sometimes come to me even today in the sounds of a storm but I am as helpless today as I was then. Gurpal was dragging me away. My *dupatta* was no longer on my head but then what hope had I of meeting *Bhaiyya* on those roads? If *Bhaiyya* had been with me, would anyone have dared touch me? Could anyone have dragged me bareheaded like this, through the paths of my birthplace where every particle was precious to us? Those paths where my father's blood was spilled. His grey hair was dragged in that dust. And if I could even catch a glimpse of that dust from his head, I'd tell that dust that it was more fortunate than I. I had so many things to say to *Baba*. How much I had irritated *Amma* and pestered *Bhai*. And when I was dragged, without a palanquin, to Sangrao, there was no mother's child to whom I could have turned to cry and lament that I was losing my parent's home with no one here to see me off. After suffering, if there's a longing for peace, and a remote hope, then the burden is lightened. And my journey was never shortened. Shall I remember or forget, Gurpal? You never let me turn my head once to have a last look.

I endured *Bari Ma*'s beatings, Gurpal's abuse, the hardship of hunger, my eye fixed on a remote hope, like a flickering lamp, that perhaps *Bhai* and *Bhaiyya* would come to Sangrao in search of me and I would smirk at *Bari Ma* and go off with my brothers, without so much as looking at Gurpal. That day the breeze, playing among the *neem* leaves, would sing anthems and the whole village would celebrate. Why do we all think ourselves the centre of the universe? Who knows? We blink in search of light until our eyes are inured to darkness and dreams. Hopes, like stray thoughts, revolve around my heart. Munni was born and the chains around my heart loosened. The troop of surrounding hopes was dispersed and I started to wake even in my dreams. Occasionally a word from me resounded in the songs of Sangrao.

When the two countries reached agreement, Gurpal was depressed, subdued and worried. He and *Bari Ma* sat in the courtyard talking about who knows what. But neither said anything to me. In those days

Munni toddled and lisped – the news flew noisily and settled, like a whirlwind. No army came to fetch me.

Then I heard that the other country's soldiers had sought out their girls and were taking them back. Where, to which country, after all? To which people?, I'd wondered at the time. Perhaps *Bhai* and *Bhaiyya* will come looking for me. They'd been expecting me for ages at the door of the magic land. I should go, definitely. I gathered the bundle of my hopes each day and look longingly at the turn at the end of the street.

That year in winter, the soldiers came to Sangrao to fetch me. Besides being *Bhai* and *Bhaiyya*'s sister, I'm also Munni's mother. And I wondered, 'Who knows who these people are, what that land is like?' For the first time in my life, my faith faltered. The land of my dreams crumbled to dust and vanished from in front of me. My roots have dug deep into the soil of Sangrao. Who ever wants to dry up, wither and be destroyed? Every girl has to leave her parents' home and go to her husband's. Every bride marries and moves elsewhere. So what, if *Bhaiyya* and *Bhai* weren't present at my departure? Gurpal had spread a welcome-carpet of corpses for me, reddened my path with blood, sacked town upon town to make fireworks for my wedding. People had celebrated my bridal night with screams and shouts and toing and froing. The whole atmosphere was infused with the smell of dust and smoke and blood, in accordance with the new traditions. He had brought me to Sangrao, among the fields of wheat, to a mud cell where I would spend the rest of my life in a house filled with the blue smoke of cow dung.

How long I had looked, after all these years, at the words on the pages of the book that Gurpal brought to read to Munni. And the words throbbed in my eyes. I suddenly recalled the stories *Bhaiyya* and *Bhai* had told me, saying, '*Bibi*, there are books with even better tales than these. Just get older and you'll see what enjoyable things there are to read.' When the army came to rescue me like the princess of fairytales, I hid. Why should I go with someone strange?, I ask you. Why aren't *Bhaiyya* and *Bhai* here to collect me and see me off? Inside,

I grew disheartened with them. I'm still upset.

As Munni lies beside me, she asks, 'Ma, why don't you go to *Mama*'s house, even at Diwali? Why doesn't *Mama* ever send us sweets?'

Mama didn't even set out to find me, Munni. They never came to rescue me. Who can find time to wander in search of someone else? Slowly, love finds crutches. *Bhaiyya*'s kids must be Munni's age. When they ask about visiting their *Mama*, he won't have to change the subject as I do, to keep a secret. Sometimes there are stories inside which can't be brought to the tongue. So, when the brides of this street work their spinning wheels, singing songs in the shade of the *neem* trees, I keep quiet.

How much life there was in our courtyard! How much sweetness there is in parental melodies. The seasons change. Year on year, fathers and brothers come to see off the brides, and Asha, Rekha, Purna and Chandra's feet don't stay on the ground. Their words sound like songs. Seasons keep changing.

The girls come out of their rooms and ask about their brothers' arrival. My heart beats in my throat and a nerve strains near my heart – it might burst. I extend my hand to chase away a crow and it falls dead beside me. *Bari Ma* has hopes of me. When I broke all links with my past life, *Bari Ma* and I formed a deeper bond. I have become her Lakshmi Bahu, her lucky daughter-in-law. She shows off the yarn spun by me with great affection. And when other women complain about their daughters-in-law, she spurs their resentment by singing my praises.

The fragrance of the grain meandering through the fields and the scent of the moist young wheat blend with the blue smoke and become a song – the sheltering sky filled with stars, single or in pairs, and the water in the spring, twisting into tiny waves, are all its words. If one day a youthful rider arrives, behind the peasants carrying bundles of fodder on their heads for the bullocks, and dismounts by my open doors, I will cry, '*Bhaiyya*!' and hug him. Who have I stood waiting for at this door? How long after the death of my dear ones must I carry the corpses? Looking at these tortuous roads, the tears start spontaneously to my eyes.

If these tears fall on Munni, she'll get up, anxious, and ask, 'Ma, why are you crying?' How will I explain my grief to Munni if she asks, 'Ma, why are your eyes wet, even on Dusehra night? Are you tired?'

Gurpal has hoisted both boys onto his shoulders. Munni and I are going to Sangrao. Sita has accepted Ravana's sanctuary, instead of a second exile. From where can I muster a second bout of incredulity to use as a crutch to support my faith?

The lights of life have distanced themselves from me like the lights of that town behind me, but I'm still unable to love the darkness, who knows why?

I've got to keep walking. Exhaustion is like a pain in every part of my body. But still, I've got to keep walking. In life's fair, exiles and grove-dwellers are forced to move on and I comply, wondering if *Bhai* and *Bhaiyya* were ever sad for me.

I'm most scared of Munni. Tomorrow she'll ask me the question again, and again no one will be able to answer it. Not Gurpal, nor I, nor, probably, *Bari Ma*.

Why are so many questions like that, so onerous and difficult, they can't be answered by anyone?

The long winter night's pain kindles a fire and recalls old dreams and listens to tales. Tell me, can tales be true? My heart is so wilful it won't forget the past.

Is there any knowledge beyond Sangrao?

In the high and low streets of the village, the stench of urine and cow dung, mixed with the smell of grain, flows on with life's torrent. Today is over. The days end like gusts of wind. Who knows how much of the journey remains?

Translated by Shahrukh Husain

Farkhanda Lodhi

Parbati

'Kill!' Was it a voice or an echoing memory?

'Kill!' It was advancing.

Guns roared . . . from both sides, from every side . . . and all round was the reverberating, recurring patriotic anthem.

'Kill!'

Cannon, aeroplanes, sirens, whistles and the thumping of hearts. Then silence. Churning the silence, dividing consciousness, a cry.

'Kill!'

A bullet whistled by, barely scraping her shoulder. Protecting her head, she bent over and started walking. The border was a few steps away. She had to get there. No sound but a hissing silence, a storm in the heart and a rumbling at the core of the earth. She tightened her grip on both arms.

Another bullet came from one side, from all sides. Rain, noise, fire, heat, thirst . . .

She inched forward, clasping her ears with both hands. Balanced and supported on her arms, she crossed the border before dawn broke. The rumble of the cannon had stopped – but now it grew louder and more rapid. There was still time for the day to break. The distinctive smell of gunpowder surrounded her, the smoke momentarily obscured the morning light.

She lay down in the cover of the bushes and tried to breathe deeply. There was no danger of anyone passing by here. 'If I hear the sound of footsteps or see anyone coming, I'll jump into the canal on the right', she decided with complete calm. For a long time she lay lost in thought, biting her painful, swollen lips. She had so many obstacles to face. The wounds on her knees were oozing fresh blood and she was aware of her chest wounds, stiff with caked dirt. 'Where can I go in this condition?' her mind kept reflecting.

The morning birds had not begun their chorus. Why were they silent? Fire and thunder had swallowed their happy contentment and the world appeared desolate. How quickly the world's beauty had changed to mourning. She was choked by fear and hatred. A wave of revulsion, towards loved ones, strangers, even her own being, ran through her. Her inner self plunged into deeper and deeper darkness. The sun refused to come up. Cannon-balls thundered and the horizon was lit by temporary flares that would illuminate the sky and then suddenly die down. Each time she heard the rumble she feared a cannon-ball would land on her. She had chosen a bad spot to stop. Danger was imminent. She moved forwards. Further and further. The dread silence moaned palpably and shouted out, as children were orphaned and widowed women's precious honour was plundered. The rumble of tanks and cars, slogans old and new, noise . . . People awoke and involved themselves in life's struggles, but her mind was still asleep. Totally paralysed. How could she go among those people? She was almost naked, covered in blood. Her shirt hung in tatters from her breast. Ashamed of her condition, she hesitated for a fraction and then moved forward with renewed determination.

She became conscious of her wounds throbbing; her awareness grew as she emerged slowly from an unconscious state. Now she was able to register the world of objects around her. The trees standing like spirits in the semi-darkness were really trees and the sun had yet to rise. Despite the smoke, it had risen. The world has to go about its business. In the nearby village, death challenged life and life answered back, resolutely making its way forward. It cannot stop. It must not stop.

She kept walking. The village was a few paces away. Not even an ant was visible; the mistreated and angry village curs were barking. Where had the people gone? Silence gripped all. She had reached the village boundaries.

Nothing was visible behind the fallen wall. There was nothing in the village to hold back the people. She wanted to weep: over the devastation in the village, over man's helplessness and short-sightedness, or then to return to where she had come from and never set foot in this place again. There was a fierce desolation in her. She thought: The earth is our mother and look at the flames engulfing her breasts . . . why does she not die? Her sons destroy her, are destroyed themselves, and yet the air resounds with a single cry: 'Kill!'

This is the game thought up by your wise sons. O, Mother! Maybe I will get killed in this game. If I live I will think long and hard of your condition. I don't have the time now. Elastic time shrinks and expands, as in a game.

A hundred yards away the military jeeps were visible as they arrived and departed. All around were clouds of dust and smoke. Scraps of dry grass were ablaze. The standing ears of grain had been scorched and bony sticks from the old leafless tree were crackling in the flames. She wet her lips with her tongue. How thirsty she was! She would not survive. Her throat prickled with thistles. She was parched. She collapsed half alive on the mound of rubble. The sound of footsteps . . . closer . . . closer . . . and closer still and a voice telling somebody, 'Kill her!'

'Yes, yes. Kill her!'

She sat up with lightning speed and tried unsuccessfully to clothe her body. In front of her were two armed soldiers, staring at her meaningfully. Their probing looks went straight through her garments, entering her flesh, searching her mind and her heart. Her body stiffened in fear and apprehension of danger. Her power of speech had been usurped and her pupils felt as if they had turned to stone.

'Why did you not leave with the village folk? Your condition is not good.' Their tone reassured her. There were tears in her eyes.

'What . . . what can I say? I have saved myself from those savage beasts in the last village. I have faced cruelty and violence to mingle with the earth of my land. You are my brothers. Finish me. Do me this favour.' She spoke effortlessly and the soldiers were in a quandary: should they silence this talking parrot or allow her to die with her tale of woe locked in her? One of them went running off and returned with a thick cotton blanket, covering her body with it. The soldiers were restless, hesitating to make her fresh, beautiful body their target. Fire was raining down. The air was smouldering.

'Do you have any relatives?' one asked.

'Let it be, *yaar*. Don't waste time.' The other shook his head.

'Life or death?' The first one persisted.

'Whatever you can give.' There was a note of challenge in her tone now and her voice was clear.

'That is in God's hands.'

The soldier looked back. His companion had long since left. He set off without another word. She was saved. She lay among a hail of cannon and gunpowder . . . nobody came to either rescue or finish her off. The defenders of her country were fighting. Could anything be more reassuring than that?

The afternoon went by. She was worn out by thirst and hunger. A small caravan stopped near her with its token presence of men, the women and children strangely subdued. They stood under the *sheesham* tree with terror-stricken faces, children crying in their mothers' laps, their lips dry and pale. Then trucks and other vehicles drove up and the military police herded them in like cattle. A man who looked like an officer gave instructions in low tones. There was not the slightest fatigue visible on his face as he looked confidently around him. The soldiers were going about their work swiftly, their briskness and jokes relieving the atmosphere of sadness. The officer standing next to an old woman said, 'Ma! Running away from death, are you? Why don't you stay back? Let a useful man take your place.' He laughed.

'Oh no, son', she screamed in her vernacular. 'I'll tuck myself into a corner.'

'Is life that precious?'

'Yes, son, I don't want to die at the hands of those kafirs. Death will visit all one day.'

'Ma! This is a chance for martyrdom,' the soldier told the old woman.

'Martyrdom is a result of one's actions, son! I am useless. What martyrdom is there for me?'

Everyone was laughing and work continued as if nothing had happened, as if people had woken up from a night's sleep to find that the morning had dawned on a new age, a new world, and the desire to discover this new world, and apprehension at what they might find, had distracted them all. The women were silent, fear lurking in their eyes. The joy and verve of the men concealed a deep anxiety which compelled the officer to repeatedly look towards the east and the soldiers to herd the women and children like cattle.

She was wounded so she was made to lie down in a jeep. Her face wore the pallor of death and she was being removed to a hospital so she could be revived. She shouted profanities.

'Kill me . . . no, no . . . kill me . . . how will I face my own? . . . no, no . . . I am not in a position to return . . . my brother will commit suicide when he sees me . . . how will my mother show her face to anyone? I beseech you in the name of the honour of your women . . . for the sake of your wives' chastity and loyalty, leave me here. Savage beasts have plundered me. Let dogs tear me to pieces. I have no one to call my own now. I don't even belong to myself.'

She kept babbling and the jeep kept driving at full speed. The two sitting in front paid no heed to her nonsense, treating her like a piece of baggage. It was their responsibility to deliver her to her destination and that was all. The jeep stopped and one man got out. His place was taken up by empty cartons and bundles. The road was full of people. Their emotions brimmed over in the slogans they were shouting. Young boys poked their heads into the jeep and stared and she thought irritably, why doesn't the jeep start? Why was she being transported in this manner? Was it her funeral procession?

'This is my funeral procession . . .' She raised her voice and was enraged by the lack of feeling in the man sitting in the front seat. He was refusing to hear her. Has everyone turned to stone? What has happened to all of them? They've all become puppets, puppets manipulated by time and politics, she thought, and screamed at the man sitting near her, 'Are you deaf?'

'I don't have the time.'

She got up and bent over the front seat. 'You don't have the time? Not even the time to get rid of me?'

The man driving the jeep turned round to look and felt her breath on his temples. 'I won't get rid of you,' he said deliberately, 'because you're young and not bad-looking.' Then he changed the subject. 'Why don't you lie down? Don't add to my problems.'

She had come to ask him questions, talk to him, and here she was being told off. The jeep kept grinding on. The fresh air revived her slightly. 'What will you do with me?'

'Pickle you.'

She kept quiet. There was no reason to say anything further.

The jeep entered the compound of a huge building and stopped. Bearers came forward with a stretcher. She descended, spurning all help.

'All right. *Salaam.*' She stopped.

'*Wa 'eikum 'asalaam.*' The man had put on a pair of dark glasses and was looking at her: a woman wrapped in a cotton blanket, encrusted with dirt, hair in disarray and tears streaking the filthy face. She looked like a mad woman.

'What's your name?' The man's heart filled with sympathy and pity for the solitary woman.

'Nothing . . .'

'Nothing is no name.'

'Parveen', she answered shortly, lost in thought.

'Parveen', the man repeated and added, 'Peena'.

She smiled interrogatively, as if to say, 'What is my destination now?'

The man took off his dark glasses and gave her a deep look. 'I'm Hassan. Anything I can do for you?'

'Nothing . . .', Parveen answered angrily. She had been disappointed in Hassan. A strange disappointment.

'All right. *Khuda hafiz*'. Hassan walked away.

'*Khuda hafiz*'. Parveen's hand kept waving for a while. She had softened towards him again and people looked with surprise at this peasant woman with the appearance of a *sadhu*, who stood there waving goodbye in such a courteous manner till the jeep was out of view. But there was terror on her face. Pure terror.

When she recovered her health she was transferred from the hospital to the camp. She was irritated when people inquired about her close ones and relatives, turning hysterical on occasions, as if her inner world had been trampled by its experience of terror and injustice. Gradually people stopped asking.

In the camp Parveen attached herself to a widow who loved her like her own daughter. She would spend her whole day in the camp educating the women and children and people would look at her pityingly. She became everyone's *apa*. In the morning and evening it was usual for her to sit down with the younger children, who enjoyed their pupillage under her. Anxious mothers, dislocated from their homes, got some respite and they would sit and speculate in Punjabi with each other.

'*Hai nee*, what a nice girl! What will become of her?', one would ask.

The other woman, overly emotional and sensitive to Parveen's condition, would strike her breast with both hands and exclaim, 'Oh, why did the kafirs plunder her honour?'

In the camp young girls were being married off every day. Those women who are always on the lookout to marry off all the young girls in the world were on the lookout for a mate for Parveen, but to marry her required courage. The youthful male gaze would chase her the whole day – to escape it, Parveen would complete her daily tasks and, before the evening shadows darkened, leave for the fields and sit perched on the raised boundaries, lost for hours in unknown thoughts. Her eyes would search the distance . . . then she would return, head bowed, silent, her undulating walk suggestive of a *sadhu* returning to the city from his retreat. Parveen belonged to all. Everyone would fret on her behalf. Parents would worry as she walked with her *dupatta* pulled right to her forehead and her gaze lowered, attracting the attention of the simple folk. Mature men would respectfully step aside to allow her to pass. She was now in a position to command deference.

She had no desire to achieve fame in her little camp world. She would meet the adults infrequently, spending all her time with the children. Everyone understood her needs. Those who themselves had broken hearts and whose wounds were fresh lacked the courage to probe hers.

One evening when she was returning to camp as usual, she met Zainab. She had met and befriended Zainab in the camp. Zainab was around eighteen or twenty years old, from a rural background and with a missing father. After displacement her small family had been located in the camp. She was often seen roaming outside the camp, her eyes and feet running anxiously along the pathways traversing the fields in anticipation of her father. When he returned, they could be settled somewhere and then Zainab's palms could be reddened with henna. Bad times were upon them. Mothers were always fearful, as Zainab and countless unwed young girls waited with their innumerable hidden desires for their fathers, brothers and would-be bridegrooms whose presence would ensure for them a carefree life. The daughters of Eve desire no more than this; to think beyond it is not possible for these simple village maidens. When news arrives of those who have died, they weep. When the message is of victory and life, they break into smiles. This is the extent of their emotions and their world.

Zainab blocked Parveen's path. '*Apa*, you have given up talking about your own people, but do you think they have given up searching for you? Come, there is someone waiting for you there.'

Parveen was taken aback and for a moment her sober face was shadowed by fear and terror.

'Come, why have you halted?'

Parveen took a few faltering steps. She did not address Zainab.

'*Apa*, why are you afraid? Your relatives will not devour you. It's not your fault . . .' Zainab had drawn her own conclusions from Parveen's confusion.

The earth and the sky tilted as she saw Hassan in front of her. The universe began to destruct. There was one thought in her mind: 'Why has he come? Why has he come? Why has he come?'

Without lifting her eyes or replying to Hassan's greeting, she stood trembling. Her resolve had abandoned her, she had no idea that she would prove to be so weak. Gradually her lips opened and her eyes lifted. '*Salaam*.'

'Why are you so disturbed?'

'I'm all right.'

Then Hassan began talking. 'I went to the hospital for some work one day. I asked about you and was told that you had been sent to camp. I happened to be passing this way today and here you are. That is good.' He spoke in clipped sentences.

'Yes, I'm delighted . . .' Parveen responded formally. Zainab had left.

'You recognize me, don't you? You remember my name?' Hassan asked again.

'Yes, well . . . very well.'

Hassan kept quiet for a while and then spoke: 'I don't know why I get the feeling that you're a riddle and I want to decipher this riddle. Although I have no right. Even then . . .'

Parveen smiled and gave Hassan the kind of look only a woman can. She forgot what she was about to say to him. Her eyes were quizzical. Then she said, 'For a man each new woman is a riddle. Well, let's talk of something else.' Her tone was refined.

'Parveen, I want to talk to you. Not of war. War is the scourge of God. I want to talk of forgiveness and mercy. I want to dream about peace and friendship with you . . .'

Then Hassan kept quiet. Parveen was also silent. The stillness spoke and they listened and understood.

'All right. I'll go now. I'll come again, God willing . . .', he said as he left. Parveen, in a quandary, stood rooted to the spot, staring.

Hassan would come for short visits. They would sit in a grove, sharing each other's life stories and the happenings in the world. Parveen talked about her failures and incompetence and sought to convince Hassan of them. It was extremely worrying that Hassan was pursuing her. She would often think of what Hassan was looking for in her. Still, somewhere in Parveen's heart and the deepest recesses of her soul, there was a hidden happiness which, despite her efforts, would spill from her eyes and which Hassan would recognize. Parveen's mind would not accept this happiness. She was not convinced of it.

While recounting an incident from his childhood, Hassan said to her, 'Look, Peena, there are some matters in which one always remains a child. I think I'm still a child. When I was about five or six I would play in the lane outside. At times one can acquire wonderful things in play, can't one?'

He wanted the listener's assent while telling his story. Parveen, absorbed in the tale, had forgotten her role.

'God takes good care of human innocence. One day I found a pearl, coated in mud and dirt. So beautiful and lovely . . . at least it appeared that way to me. I cleaned it with spit and polished it on my shirt front. How it sparkled! Then I put it in my mouth and played with it. Peena! I still haven't understood, why does one want to swallow the things one likes best? There is a spontaneity in a child's desire which adults learn to repress. But the desire for spontaneity remains. I remember my mother scolded me for this antic and even slapped me. She would say, "Heaven knows what filth he picks up and pops into his mouth." I sobbed for such a long time, clutching the pearl in my fist. Why did Mother not respect my desire? My tiny consciousness came awake that day and I shed tears of blood. I persuaded my elder sister to sew the pearl on the collar of my coat and hugged it close to me for many days. Perhaps others didn't like it but I was very happy.'

Parveen showed her appreciation of this unimportant event with tiny chuckles and Hassan was revived by the continuous magic of her femininity, falling on him as lightly as rain.

The neighbouring country had unexpectedly attacked in the night, violating all established norms and practices. Many fronts had been opened up and Hassan had to run from one to another. The army was small and the size of the enemy substantial. One man had to do the work of four. Hassan was a lieutenant, and as in this war more officers were being martyred, Parveen began to fear for Hassan's life and pray for him, 'Let Hassan return safely. Make sure he does.'

She sometimes felt as if Hassan was her purpose in life and beyond that purpose there was no other world. He talked a lot whenever he came: his men were pushing back the enemy on all fronts, the enemy was being defeated, and so on. Parveen would sit silently staring at the sky, unmoved by the result. She could hear nothing beyond the sound of Hassan's voice.

Hassan was wounded in the arm by a bullet and got fifteen days leave so he took Parveen home. He was living in the midst of love and war, unmindful of what was permitted and what was not. It is death to retreat in conditions of love or war. Hassan was not prepared either to die physically or face the death of his love. His country was winning the war and it was his personal goal to win his love. A few days later Hassan got married.

On her wedding day, Parveen imposed a silence on herself and sat lost in it. Despite Hassan's insistence, she couldn't describe her feelings. Then slowly a complete change came over her. She turned her entire attention to the home, laughing and chirping the whole day. This was Hassan's home. It was her home. When Hassan was on duty she would sit on the prayer mat saying all kinds of prayers. She had texts framed from the revealed scriptures and the sayings of the Prophet and hung them on all the walls of the house. When Hassan came home he would find her increasingly drawn to religion. Parveen's reactions forced Hassan to wonder about her more and more. A barely educated, average, middle-class woman living in a small community, what does she think and why does she behave this way? Why does she read religious and scholarly tracts? Why is she, in this day and age, becoming more and more obsessed with religion? And yet, as the rituals and ablutions to purify and cleanse grew, Parveen's face became more fresh and radiant. Soon, peace was declared and the land revealed itself in the form of a mother.

At teatime Parveen appeared different to Hassan. He began to look at her, embarrassing her with his unblinking gaze. Then he took her in his lap and she buried her face in his breast, till it seemed as if the entire universe was confined within the single, shared, warm breath of Hassan and Parveen. Eyes bathed in the clear springs of emotion sparkled, each was spellbound. Hassan broke it by asking, 'Peena, why are you turning so religious? I'm astonished.'

'I am trying to thank my Creator who has given me so much.' Parveen spoke with difficulty. 'Given me so much.' She kept repeating under her breath, 'Given me so much, given me . . .'

Hassan looked into her eyes and smiled. 'What has He given you?' he asked mischievously.

Parveen shyly lowered her eyes.

'Oh, I see!' And he kissed and kissed her eyes, drenching her in a shower of trust and intimacy. Like the morning star a single word pulsed in her mind: 'Victory . . . victory . . . victory . . .'

In spring the quality of air changes. Hassan got two promotions in quick succession. He attributed his success to Parveen's lucky star. This woman was fortunate and her honest presence ensured a bright future for him, Hassan became Parveen's worshipper. This soft-limbed, dusky woman ruled over his senses, his heart and his home simultaneously. Her behaviour and her handling of household matters had so overwhelmed Hassan that he was no longer mindful of the world. Parveen combined in her person all the roles of a woman. Like a mother she knew how to upbraid him, she could tease and indulge him like a sister, and offer sacrifices and take pride in him like a wife.

After his promotion Hassan was posted to another city and he moved with Parveen to a new house, far away from the world which had made her acquaintance. Both were pleased with the change. The routine of their nights and days altered and then a flower was soon to bloom in their own garden. Could anyone be more fortunate than Hassan? Peaceful days and the richness of life surged all around him.

At the breakfast table, finding that Hassan was not in his usual high spirits, Parveen became anxious. Since their marriage he had not been quiet for a moment. His eyes looked burdened. Parveen felt a deep dread. 'Hassan, what has happened to your eyes? Why are they so burdened?'

Hassan put down his cup on the table and remained silent. He still didn't look at Parveen. She grabbed him by both arms and shook him, nearly at the point of tears herself. 'Why are you silent? Why don't you tell me . . .?'

'I wasn't able to sleep at night,' Hassan said in a feeble voice.

'Why?' Parveen asked impatiently. 'Why didn't you wake me up?'

'I was hardly awake myself, I don't know what state I was in. I kept having the most horrifying dream. I have been weeping since then.'

Hassan threw his head back and looked at the ceiling. His eyes grew wet again. Hassan and tears? Parveen was amazed. This man who has played in blood on the battlefield, who has witnessed bodies piled before his eyes and triumphantly leapt over them as the victorious warrior, the courageous and brave soldier, can he be so weak and delicate?

'Tell me the dream. It'll lighten your burden.'

'Why do you want to hear it, it'll cause you pain . . .'

'You have to tell me.'

Hassan began to speak haltingly. 'There's a garden and it's springtime', he said thoughtfully, as if he was pasting snapshots in an album and recalling forgotten names. His voice had deepened.

'Two birds had lost their way and I built them a nest in which they began to live happily. Then somehow the nest caught fire, and their children were also in the nest. Peena . . .' He stopped. 'The blaze grew and I stood weeping. When I awoke my pillow was wet. I was burdened, as if I had set fire to the nest with my own hands. I am the guilty one who has caused the fire and consigned everything to the flames. I was not able to go back to sleep.'

Parveen was lost listening to the story and waves of anguish swept over her face. She sat silent and trembling. Last night, half-asleep, she had heard the sound of Hassan's footsteps and felt him bending over her face many times, and then she had turned over and gone back to sleep. Now Hassan was telling the story and everything in the house was suddenly quiet and sombre.

Neither of them spoke to each other till Hassan's departure for the office. A heavy fear blanketed their hearts and they were hesitant to see each other's faces. Can people all of a sudden turn into distant strangers, like uncertain, faceless shadows? Time's slate reflected two such shadows: trembling, helpless and sorrowful.

As he left, Hassan reminded her, 'Be ready. Today we'll go for a long drive. I don't want that horrifying dream to be repeated tonight. Maybe walking around will make me feel better. You're looking tired as well.' He stooped to kiss Parveen on the forehead on his way out and then left without doing so. There was a determination in his stride which had been absent earlier. Parveen felt a twinge and then a wave of unknown hope and longing swept over her.

They set out for their outing in the early evening. Hassan was driving the jeep himself. The early evening moon shifted slowly to the west. Parveen sat quietly, clutching her locket in her fist, lost in thought. Hassan had brought her the locket this evening; on the little tablet was inscribed 'Allah'. God's name in her fist, and in her heart a world of danger and fear. On the way a dread stillness and Hassan's silence.

'Where are we going?' she finally asked.

'You know I always surprise you.' Hassan spoke as little as possible.

'Yes, you've always amazed me . . .' She was comforted by his response. She was so used to Hassan's ways that she did not attempt to go into any further details.

'Go to sleep.' Hassan rested her head on his shoulders. The jeep kept moving and Parveen appeared to be asleep. Hassan stopped his jeep and very carefully helped Parveen down, as if she were made of fragile glass, and supporting her, began to walk. Perhaps this was the desired destination.

It was the late evening of a chilly night. Now they were on foot. The sand was shifting beneath their feet and the moments slid slowly by.

'Where are you taking me, Hassan?' Parveen asked once more, close to tears. She was pregnant and she couldn't walk very far. Her feet were losing their grip on the sand. But Hassan was dragging her now. The desert was silent except for the wind rustling through the bushes and the sound of shifting sand. Overhead a field of stars spanned the horizon.

Hassan stopped. He held Parveen tightly to him, then kissed her and set her apart. He was panting from the journey and the heavy burden he was carrying inside him.

'Parbati! Go! *Khuda hafiz.*' He set off.

A scream escaped Parbati. The dark made it difficult for them to read each other's expressions.

'Parbati, don't forget. You have something of mine in safe keeping.' He stopped and spoke, and then his shadow disappeared behind the bushes.

'Hassan! Hassan!' Parbati ran after him and fell down. Her arms fluttered in the air, her hands pressed her mouth to stifle the cries lest they rent asunder the heart of silence. Hassan had left.

Shiv had left Parbati. Adam had pushed Eve alone out of paradise. At this moment she was neither Parbati nor Parveen, but just woman, a worshipper of love and the flower-bearing earth. She lay face down weeping on the desert and her locket with 'Allah' inscribed on it kept rolling in the sand. She was scattered by the trinity of the desert: God, Adam and Eve. Separated by politics.

'Hassan, Hassan, Hassan'. Parbati's golden dream had ended.

Night was almost over. The light of a new dawn spread its rays on the horizon. A man bending over her was saying, 'Beat her to death, *yaar.*' And with presence of mind she announced, 'I am Parbati. Colonel Mehta's wife'. She didn't want to die.

On this side of the border she was Mrs Mehta again. *Shrimati* Parbati Mehta, Colonel Mehta's wife. She had a clear dusky colouring, was petite but perfectly proportioned, and had a black mole on the left cheekbone as well as the mark of a wound aslant the brow. Her expression was sober. The government circulated her description in the newspapers and disseminated it in handbills. During the war she had set out to spy in the enemy camp. For a while she kept them informed of her whereabouts, then her world changed. Her passion and fervour, like a limpid stream, found fresh channels and a new, rich existence. This way had been opened to her by Hassan. Hassan had watered her garden. She was the mother of his unborn child. The thought of motherhood had elevated her worth in her own eyes: she felt important and splendid. She felt she had come into her own, had penetrated the secrets of her own being. She who was a person in her own right but whom people had taunted as an unproductive woman, infertile earth, her breast was full of treasures now.

When she had been married to Mehta she was very young and impulsive. Mehta gave her everything except confidence. She was convinced that it was possible to have a home even without children. Parbati was justifiably proud of the grand Colonel Mehta. Being his wife had given her a place in society but she never stopped being the victim of people's envy and greed. Then, even as now, people remained ready to marry their daughters to Colonel Mehta. Ten years of married life went by. She was a wordly, married woman of twenty-eight when she began to feel that there was much more for a woman to achieve than motherhood. She was constantly obsessed by one thought: she would achieve something before she died, she would achieve something before she died.

War broke out with the neighbouring country, and countless

mothers' precious sons began to write history with their blood. For security the frontiers demanded blood . . . fresh blood poured into human forms, borne by women and then sacrificed by them before city walls. Seeing their precious ones fall, these women could then raise their heads in pride and say, 'I have a share in this earth. I have drenched it with my blood. This fertile land is my being . . . I am earth itself. I produce these gems and I swallow them as well.'

Parbati grew more and more restless. Blood coursed through her veins, vigorous and passionate. She was perpetually conscious of her low status. She would always be deprived of the honour of adding another drop to the flowing river. A drop drawn from her blood and being. How impossible this was. She could have gained the honour by sacrificing her husband, but that appeared difficult. Without him what would she be? She thought: now that fires are raging all around and life is uncertain, I could receive the news of Mehta's death any moment. Who would she lean on after Mehta's death? She would be Mehta's widow, without a medal, honour, pension or anything. She resolved that instead of this aimless existence, she would do something to ensure her name for posterity.

When a woman cannot become a mother she has many other desires.

Mehta's love had lost its earlier centredness and abundance. Knowing each other, they still remained strangers. Mehta would busy himself with office business most of the time. The wife would occupy herself with social work. At night they would go to bed exhausted. Life had fallen into a rut and lost all meaning. But war brought a new quest and aspirations into their life. New windows opened on enchanting vistas. There were many opportunities for Parbati now. Mehta suggested that she become a nurse, but instead of bandaging other's wounds she longed to receive some herself. She longed to run to the front lines, to comfort the soldiers, to do battle and go tearing through the enemy lines. She kept badgering Mehta with this desire. The only opening he could find for her obsession was that she go and spy in enemy territory, make use of her beauty and intelligence and if she had to lay down her life, well, she desired that anyway. That would immortalize her.

An injection of morphine made her bear the wounds inflicted on her body, and for the sake of her country she crossed the frontier at night. Then her life began to change. Gradually soft-spoken Hassan entered the temple of her heart, made a place in it. They were spiritually one. After marrying Hassan, Parbati was reborn. Perhaps she had been created for Hassan and had travelled these long distances to arrive at this point. How much hardship she had undergone to make him hers and how much tyranny she had endured, only her heart knew. After gaining Hassan she had put away her past life as a time in prison which had passed in hope of freedom. Hassan was the ultimate haven after the turmoil her soul had undergone, not just a man who had given her self-confidence. She who had been a criminal in everybody's perception was now witness to her own existence, her pride, her soul and emotions . . . now she could say she was no less than anyone else. She too had an established goal.

She was picked up from the border and transported with the utmost care to Colonel Mehta. Mehta greeted her with love and courtesy, but Parbati was not the same. She was haunted by the fear that if Mehta found out he would not treat her well at all, and it was inevitable he find out. Parbati never told her husband but he gauged the situation. His eyes turned crimson with rage and he was like an angry hyena.

'I didn't expect this of you.' He was silent for a while and then said, 'For the sake of the country . . . all right . . . you had no option.' His tone softened. He remembered the sacrifices made by Parbati and allowed his head to rest on her shoulder. Parbati lay curled up on the bed, not answering any questions but watching the play of emotions on Mehta's face. She sat silent, as if she was a migrant from a faraway land who had stopped at the wayside inn for a few hours. Despite all that Mehta said, she was not conscious of any sense of guilt. She had committed no crime, she was sure. Mehta continued talking and in an attempt to console her said, 'Don't worry. We'll get rid of it.'

'You have been childless . . . we can adopt it,' Parbati advised.

'Useless seed . . . child of a *mlech* . . . I will not allow it in my home. Understand, Parbati! I have accepted you because of your love and loyalty, otherwise you're unclean . . . you'll have to get rid of it. Now, today or tomorrow.'

In a single breath Mehta had demanded, threatened and warned. He was pained at his wife's loss of honour and conscious of his deprivations. Parbati had returned from across the border with something that they had longed for. But Mehta had no part in it. And now Parbati, a lowly woman, was determined to have the upper hand over him. He could defeat her through violence. He leapt. Parbati shrieked.

'You can't do this. I won't let you do it . . .'

'I'll kill you . . .' He advanced towards Parbati, both hands raised.

'Kill me, then.'

Parbati offered her neck. She felt Mehta's blows on her breast and sat up in pain. Legs drawn up to protect her stomach, she kept taking the blows. Kicked and pummelled, her flesh, bones and coursing blood took a beating to save the life that had taken refuge in her, to protect the race of which she was the mother. She was mother and earth and frontier and beyond the frontier, life continued, generation succeeding generation. Life growing and burgeoning was to be protected. No . . . no . . . no . . . I will not let this happen.

Mehta lost, lost in every way. After this the tension between them grew. The time of confinement was drawing near. Mehta started disappearing from home for weeks. Parbati was calm in his absence. While he was away she could wait peacefully for the moment when the reward of a lifetime would be poured into her lap. Her motherhood would signify new hope, she would be overwhelmed with joy.

In Mehta's absence Parbati went to hospital. She informed neither her own family nor her in-laws but she did scribble a few lines to Mehta. It was his choice whether to maintain the relationship or break it. She had no hopes of anyone, no relationship with anyone. The whole world had disappointed her. Even Hassan. Love and emotions prosper for a while but, faced with the demands of duty or other goals, they are either throttled by others or destroy themselves. Maintaining a relationship becomes a curse. To break relationships is a worthy act and Parbati was breaking all relationships, without asking whether it was praiseworthy or not. It was just the beginning of the journey for her. She was midway. No final decision was possible at the moment. She had seen a dream, its realization was a way off. She had still to touch it with her lips. After that she will think. After that, duty will call, and she will listen and take a decision. The ultimate moment was slowly drawing closer. She was waiting with hope, arms outstretched. Time was ticking away.

New buds opened and new leaves emerged on the ancient *peepal* tree on the hospital lawn. Seasons change and protected from the strong, icy blast of winter, the new plants and buds burst forth. The earth's lap became verdant and so did Parbati's.

Bathed in dew the morning dawned.

As seasons change, the mornings are sad but heady. The sunshine is pale, neither clear nor bright, and its fresh, scrubbed beauty spreads and enters the human heart. It was the first day of spring and a new day for Parbati.

The bearer informed her that Colonel Mehta had arrived. Parbati confidently raised her head. Mehta could not break all ties with her. He was sure of a reconciliation. He thought now that he had come back things would perhaps work out. She sat with the child clasped to her breast. Mehta entered the room smiling, but instead of reflecting softness or consideration, his eyes were fiery. Fire that sends out sparks. Parbati responded to his smile with a smile of her own and sat silently.

'Let's go,' Mehta ordered on entering.

'Where?'

'Home. Where else? Come now, I've brought the car.'

'Have you gone crazy? Can't you see my child . . .'

Mehta interrupted her. 'You've driven me crazy, Parbati.' He stepped forward. 'For the sake of Bhagwan, kill these emotions. Start a new life. Learn to live with me. You have disgraced everyone. You're on a suicidal mission . . .'

Parbati didn't reply. Her mind was blank. She was not even thinking, so, meekly like a goat, she followed him. If she created a commotion in the hospital what would people have said? . . . With this thought she set out with Mehta. All the way Mehta was aloof, muttering under his breath as if in a state of intoxication.

'Parbati! You're a woman. The Muslims call a woman fire. They are right. You are a woman. Fire. You have consumed everything, burnt it to cinders. I can't even leave you. What am I to do? Parbati, Parbati! You have led Shiv astray. Humiliated him . . .'

On reaching home Parbati was given a comfortable bed. The servants had disappeared somewhere so Mehta heated the food himself and fed her warm milk and biscuits. He didn't think it necessary to explain the changes she noticed in the house and she herself was tired of playing a role. Now she wanted to sit back and watch as a spectator. There was a pleasure to it that she was just beginning to experience . . . to sit back in comfort and without a worry. Whatever will be will be. She had entrusted her ship to the waves and wanted to see what would happen.

Afternoon deepened into evening, night fell, then daybreak approached. It was time for the lamps to be dimmed and she lay with her eyes open. The whole night she was awake, eyes open, staring . . . A hand will move forward to shut out the light in her eyes now . . . now.

The night passed like a serpent that has just given birth and is in search of its young to swallow them. Who are her children? The stars . . . Parbati couldn't think too much. She has a star-like child herself and she is not going to allow anyone to swallow him up. He is a piece of the moon. He will shine. He will shine forth and be transformed into the sun . . . There was still time before sunrise. Her limbs began to relax . . . Why were her eyes drooping? Sleep. Sweet sleep. Drapes. Heavy drapes. Forgetfulness. She was dreaming. Mehta is here . . . he is searching for something by her side. The child began to cry . . . It was no dream.

Slaps . . . snatching . . . struggle between life and death . . . tears and entreaties . . . hatred. Envy and suffocation. Defeat and a sense of guilt.

'I tell you, you should kill him.' Mehta growled like a wild cat, who in its greed separates the heads of its young from their bodies.

'No. No'. She sobbed and hid her child beneath her breasts. She would defend him in every way. Her body was enough.

'I'll leave as soon as it's morning . . . go far away.' She was trembling with passion even as she made this confident assertion, panting out the words in smouldering rage. After that she lost consciousness of what she did. She left home.

Before the evening shadows deepened she found herself walking toward the border. A storm of emotions had driven her crazy. A madwoman was walking on the breast of the earth. Mother earth. A unifying entity, a common human possession.

She had forgotten that there are countries on this earth and countries have borders and borders are guarded. She walked on.

In front of her the sun sank slowly, very slowly, into the ocean in the west. The earth and the sky were bathed in blood. On and on she walked, slowly . . . slowly . . . closer and closer and closer. A bullet whistled by, grazing her shoulder. Her arms tightened across her breast and she bowed her head. Another bullet . . . and then another . . . and now she had gone very far. Many voices resounded in the atmosphere . . . kill . . . bullets rained from all sides . . . a storm. So many bullets for her solitary self . . . smoke spreading. Darkness swam before her eyes. A voice, rising and falling. The soil at the border . . . her blood, red, warm, young and fresh . . . then peace, silence and the resounding echo: 'Kill!'

Translated by Samina Rahman

Umme Umara

The Sin of Innocence

It was a frosty winter morning. When she opened her eyes the train had halted somewhere and the shouts of the coolies and the sleepy voices of the vendors came from afar. She quietly raised the window and peeped out. They were at a large railway junction. A blast of chilly air made her shiver. Hastily rolling the window down, she lay on the berth willing herself to go back to sleep.

'Don't go to sleep. We've arrived.' *Amma* softly caressed her hair. This was her first experience of a long train journey. Before this, all journeys were associated with *Baba*. He laboured in faraway lands and running the home was *Amma*'s responsibility. *Amma,* his better half, proved to be so in all areas of endeavour. The children were studying in the best schools, the lands were being diligently looked after, relatives and dear ones were being attended to and nobody had occasion to complain.

Baba being away from home, *Amma* dealt with the children so that they would not miss his presence at all. She gave them so much love that, drunk on its excess, they would obey her every command, believing in the paradise that lay beneath her feet. Living their lives in ease, and without a conscious plan, they had set a future course for themselves on the road to progress. When, in a year's time, *Baba* returned home from his foreign travels and journeys in strange lands and found his garden of delight flourishing, he would be beside himself with joy.

They all loved *Baba*. His presence added to their happiness but at the same time they were afraid of him. When he was around, *Amma* would move about replete within herself. She would discuss everything on earth with him, from the family to the neighbours, and *Baba*, too, never tired of listening to her. She would bestow her advice on *Baba* at every step and he would value it. It was often seen that when *Baba* was struggling with a problem and his own reason was proving unequal to the task, *Amma* would offer her services and *Baba*, shifting his responsibility on to her, would settle back with a sigh of relief. *Amma* was the All-Knowing Intelligence and he had faith that she could never fail. There was no doubt that *Amma* was a formidable lady and the entire family trusted her farsightedness. Yet . . . yet when *Baba* returned from Bengal and announced his decision, *Amma* lost her nerve and all her headiness vanished. She would look worriedly about her, her eyes probing the very threshold and walls of the *haveli*, her hands caressing each brick as if it were the form of a loved one, or then she would round on *Baba* in angry dispute. She would try and convince him with her arguments but this time *Baba* was not in the least impressed with her far-sightedness. He would keep hammering on at the same point: that they could no longer live there. He could not remit money from where he lived, and if money could not be remitted then how were the children to be educated and children without learning are of no use, like unfashioned wood. Most important of all, he could not see any future for his children here, and the children were the sum of his life. Their well-being was his happiness.

'Then what about this *haveli*, these lands, our village and our people?' *Amma* would ask in broken tones and her voice would be swept away in a stream of tears. She would be separated from all her brothers and sisters.

'Why don't you understand? Nothing is possible here any more. These children are all we possess. Even if you desire it, there is no space for them here. You will earn nothing from these lands. It's a question of a foreign country and we cannot live here any more.'

For the first, and perhaps last time, *Amma* had to face defeat. Then they watched her sadly pack and put away her things and a storm of tears would rise in her eyes over trifling matters. Seeing *Amma's* restlessness, *Baba* would also be agitated, but she was waging an unsuccessful struggle to understand his words: how did one's own home turn into a foreign land?

This *haveli,* its threshold and walls, its spacious courtyard (which tired one to cross it from one end to the other), the sturdy *neem* and *peepal* trees under whose shade marbles are played and these three large open rooms, *Amma's* pride and joy, were places where they had lived since they had first opened their eyes. She would always say, 'My bridal palanquin came through the large gate and was placed right here, and, God willing, my bier will also leave through the same large gate. Every happily married woman cherishes this desire.'

And . . . now it was the same *Amma*, the same house, the same village. Then how did this world turn into a world of strangers? And the place where *Baba* lives, that unseen world, how has it become our country? She would turn it over endlessly in her mind but was still not able to make head or tail of it. The far end of the skein would remain as tangled as ever and having tired herself out she would listlessly creep away to sleep long hours in the loft. The other brothers and sisters would dream of a bright future as they packed and chattered and made plans for a happy tomorrow. Nobody gave her a thought and she would comfortably turn, rub her eyes and continue sleeping, when suddenly *Amma* would be reminded of her and then everything would be turned upside down. A search would be conducted from one corner of the house to all the neighbouring homes and when everyone was exhausted, *Amma*, in her anxiety, would remember the loft, and exclaim that *Munni Rani* must be in her little haven. And then *Bade Bhaiyya* or *Amma* would fetch her from there. In those days when everyone was worrying about the other, she was only concerned whether there would be a loft in *Baba's* house . . . and when *Baba* came she had repeatedly asked him whether the house they were going to had a loft or not. Instead of answering, *Baba* would smile.

Why does *Baba* fob her off with a smile instead of answering her question? There was definitely no such thing as a loft there. If there was none, then . . . then what kind of a house would it be? And how would all their belongings find a home? Thinking and struggling to draw answers from within herself, the days went by, one by one, and swallowing her tears she went on with packing. Then one day they all stood on the platform waiting for the train to carry them from the foreign land to their own country, and after a long journey of two days and two nights, she was standing on this huge platform.

The coolies had started their jostling. *Bade Bhaiyya*, in a responsible manner, was helping the orderly to get the luggage organized. It wasn't as if they were travelling light. *Amma* appeared to have carried the whole house with her. The luggage finally collected, their little cavalcade was ready to start. But she was freezing. The chill December wind had turned her feet to stone and it was difficult for her to take two steps.

'*Bade Bhaiyya*, please hire a rickshaw, I can't walk.'

'Where would one find a rickshaw here, Bibi? A *tum-tum* is available though,' a coolie said in passing.

'So let's take a taxi. What do you think, *Bade Bhaiyya*?' She didn't fancy a *tum-tum*.

'Really, child! There isn't even a rickshaw here and you're asking for a taxi.' The orderly had been listening to her conversation.

'Then how will I walk? My feet are numb.' She looked helplessly at *Bade Bhaiyya*.

'Come, little one, I'll pick you up,' he said, gathering her in his arms.

'Hush. Do you think I'm a child?' She wiggled out of *Bade Bhaiyya*'s arms.

Ever since her eldest sister had been married she had become very conscious of her years. Whenever someone dismissed her as a child, her reaction would be extreme and she would try to impress her adult status on them.

'Then, child, I suggest you take quicker strides. See – like I do. Then you won't feel cold.' The orderly walked past her rapidly. *Bade*

Bhaiyya followed suit. Trying to keep up, she also quickened her pace and stepped off the platform onto a gravel road. Its crunch underfoot jolted her. Why had *Baba* lied? He had said that the roads here were so lovely and shining that a person could even see their face in them. How was she to know that love transmutes dirt into gold and transforms a stone into a mirror? How *Baba* loved this soil . . . but this was something she was not aware of till much later. She had contented herself then with the observation that *Baba* could also lie on occasion and this revelation had been chalked up to experience and nothing else. Hurrying down the road she had loved its gravelly sensation. That frost-wrapped winter morning still glowed in the recesses of her memory. What new experiences she'd had that morning! Walking on the road had brought a strange sense of freedom. In her village they were carried about in a palanquin and there was not the claustrophobic rush of rickshaws here either. Going down the gravel road that morning she had experienced a rush of happiness, timeless in quality, that was still alive within her. The gentle mist, the damp smell of earth, the feel of dew on the feet and the slippery crunch of gravel underfoot. All of this was completely new for her and full of exciting smells, and when, her heart welling with happiness, she had arrived at the place where their small cavalcade had stopped and the coolies were laying down their loads, she had seen *Baba*. All wrapped up in a Kashmiri shawl, his tall presence loomed magnetically before her.

'*Baba*, it's me!' She clung to him.

'My daughter!' *Baba* bent to kiss her. 'Where have you left *Amma* and your other brothers and sisters?'

'They're all behind. Only I ran to reach you.' She panted happily, looking all around. *Baba* got busy talking to *Bade Bhaiyya* and issuing instructions to the orderly about the luggage.

She examined the house she was standing in front of carefully. This was a new type of house. Tall and with a large compound, it was surrounded by verandahs in front and at the back and had nothing like a courtyard around. The entire compound had been enclosed with a prickly-barbed wire fence.

This was their house! How different it was from their *haveli*. There their *haveli* had an immense courtyard and in it had stood *neem* and *peepal* trees, and such lovely guava trees as well, and here . . . here along with the sturdy mango, *jaman* and jack fruit, the tall coconut and beetlenut trees swayed overhead. The damp fragrance of earth pervaded the humid air as she looked, in the shivering electric light, at the house which was now her abode. That was a *haveli*, and this . . . this was bungalow no. T/80! She took a deep breath and her mind filled with the familiar scent of *harsinghar*.

'*Baba, Baba*.' She ran to him as he stood, deep in conversation with *Amma*, his arms around *Choke Bhaiyya*.

'*Baba*, look here as well, I mean there's that lovely scent here too!' she said happily.

'Yes, child. This is the scent of the *harsinghar*. Here they also call it *sheoli*.'

Sheoli or *harsinghar*, *harsinghar* or *sheoli*, what difference does it make? The story of the journey from *harsinghar* to *sheoli* is a long one. She asked her father countless times, 'Why *sheoli*? Why not *harsinghar*?'

'Because, my child, here, in this part of your land, *harsinghar* is *sheoli*,' *Bade Bhaiyya* chipped in.

'And because you have to live and die in this land, therefore you will have to accustom yourself to calling it *sheoli* and not *harsinghar* . . . That was your past and this is your present and only if you live in the present will you be able to build a promising future for yourself. So, Munni child, my advice to you is to give more importance to your future than to the past.'

'Listen, *Bade Bhaiyya*, I don't agree with you. Tell me, how is it possible to build a relationship with the future, or dream dreams of a bright tomorrow, by forgetting the past? When one has no memory of the past, how can one love the present and . . .?'

'Forget it. Your mind is filled with straw. Actually you're prejudiced.'

'*Bade Bhaiyya*, my not speaking Bangla is not such a crime that you should accuse me of prejudice. I just can't break the habit of speaking my own language.'

'What do you mean? I haven't understood.'

'I mean, my dear *Bade Bhaiyya*, that when I can get by through speaking my own language, why should I commit the sin of distorting another perfectly good language by speaking it incorrectly? Don't you agree, *Baba*? It's not in me to speak a language incorrectly . . .' She laughed.

'And since when has English become your mother tongue, that you are pursuing it with a vengeance?' *Bade Bhaiyya* was peeved. 'You're always showing off, even if you don't know the first thing about it . . .'

'God forbid that English should be my language, and the only reason I'm pursuing it is that people like you may not brand me as ignorant. And as far as speaking it incorrectly goes, I have no qualms about ruining it. It's not a sign of our emancipation, but a token of our servitude, and obviously one does not love such tokens. Understood, *Bade Bhaiyya*?' She looked at him ironically.

'Not to learn the language of the place one lives in, that's unfair.'

'Who's refusing to learn it? I'm just not interested in speaking it like an ignoramus.'

'And why have I started to speak correct Urdu then?' Pakhi intervened.

'That's because Urdu is my language,' chirped *Bade Bhaiyya*.

'You're labouring under a misapprehension.' Pakhi smiled at *Bade Bhaiyya*.

'Deny, if you can, that Urdu is the language of love.' *Bade Bhaiyya* smiled back.

'As far as Munni *Bitiya* is concerned, is our language even worse than English so that she will pile sins on herself if she speaks it?' Pakhi had taken her words amiss.

'Oh no, Pakhi. Who said that? Not at all! Your language is the largesse that freedom bestowed on us, otherwise how removed we would have been from it. It's as dear to us as our own mother tongue . . .' She tried to make amends.

'And me . . .?'

'It's another matter for you, Pakhi *rani*. Have I, like you, exchanged vows of love . . .?' she laughed.

'This is wrong, Munni child. You don't praise her for her courage, but turn around and make fun of her.'

'You are there to praise her.'

The whole business of praise stretched to such lengths that, quite unobtrusively, both pronunciation and language changed: from '*pakas*' to '*phirni*' and from '*phirni*' to '*firni*'. From '*sharm ata hai*' (the masculine gender) to '*sharm ati hai*' (the feminine gender). Once when *Bade Bhaiyya* took her to Patna to show her glimpses from his past he had entertained the entire clan and, according to Pakhi, they had all liked her a lot. She would take great pleasure in saying, 'In our part of the world', 'In my in-laws' home', 'In our Patna' and 'When we went to Allahabad we saw the confluence of the Ganga and Jamuna just like the Sheeta Alekha and Deheleshwari embracing each other.'

'Yes, just the way you embraced me.' *Bade Bhaiyya* laughed and Pakhi blushed. She found Pakhi's blushes a little strange. In this part of the world even brides are quite assertive. *Bade Bhaiyya*'s faith that 'slowly everything will settle down' turned out to be correct. Sure enough, gradually, everything did settle down. Pakhi had not only married *Bade Bhaiyya* but his language, his ways, his customs and traditions had become her own.

Bade Bhaiyya was so lost in Pakhi that he quite forgot himself, and Pakhi, with the greatest of ease, kept adding one person after another to the family numbers.

Amma and *Baba*, who had initially had very little interest in her person and had tolerated her membership of the family as an unpleasant duty, were delighted with her astonishing fecundity, and the same house that had been seen as spacious became the epitome of cramped living. Two rooms in bungalow no. T/80 were under the exclusive control of Pakhi, and her little princes and princesses ruled over the remaining three rooms as well. One room had been designated the drawing room, but in name only. Its actual condition was such that a baby's dummy lay in one place and a bottle of milk in another. Someone would be clutching the divan and reciting the alphabet, because there was nothing else to amuse the young master in that room. Elsewhere, Rani and Baby's books were being reduced to pulp. When, for his sins, *Chote Bhaiyya* visited Dhaka in his vacations, his booklets and notebooks would be torn to shreds. At least she felt this way.

Who was she? A slender, tawny young girl, solitary even while living in the midst of all, loving life and fragrances of all kind, courageous despite her deceptively slim being and with the ability to take on mountains if necessary. But in this house *Bade Bhaiyya* was no less than a mountain and Pakhi, with her seven little ones, was, as it were, its summit. And she was never able to take them on. She loved *Bade Bhaiyya*, whose clear and lively intelligence had encouraged her to love life and enjoy its pleasures, who valued the brighter rather than the darker side of life and who, having once understood something, was prepared to lay down his life for it – as he was for Pakhi, who, in turn, had understood that for her salvation lay in creating a safe haven for themselves.

So she cleaned out a small outhouse in which *Amma* stored odds and ends for herself, and after days of hard work sat in it weaving together her dreams and thoughts when Pakhi dropped in and, chatting of this and that, suddenly expressed surprise. 'Don't you feel suffocated in this dark outhouse, Munni child? Like *Bade Bhaiyya* she addressed her as 'Munni child', although initially Pakhi had been her friend. It was a fact though that the friendship could not have taken on the shape that Pakhi's friendship with *Bade Bhaiyya* had assumed. Even now when she looked back she was very conscious of the transformation of *Bade Bhaiyya*.

Bengali women are sorceresses. Don't go to Bengal. From childhood this was the burden of the songs she'd heard and after settling here she had witnessed it: *Bade Bhaiyya*'s marriage to Pakhi was a successful demonstration of Bengali magic.

'*Arrey*, Munni *beta*, lost in a reverie are you? Where have you disappeared to? What have I been asking you?' Pakhi grabbed her shoulder and shook it.

She looked at Pakhi inquiringly without answering her.

'*Arrey*, I'm asking how you don't suffocate in this humidity.' She retched.

What a difference there was between that Pakhi and this Pakhi, she thought, without paying much attention to her. She had spoken in distant tones. To make obeisance and touch feet and now . . .! Yes, this is the magic that Bengali women know. Then how could this magic not hold sway? She fixed her gaze on Pakhi, who had blossomed as a result of becoming the mother of so many children. The tresses that had reached her waist now hung well below it. With her sari tied in the way *Amma* tied hers and her head covered with its end, she was another being.

'Oho, Munni child, for whose sake have you renounced the world and taken to this closed, claustrophobic room?' She shook her by the shoulder again.

'You've really learnt to talk a lot, haven't you?'

'Yes, why not? After all my children . . .' She retched violently. 'Oh God, this heat! My head is spinning.'

'You mean . . .' She looked at Pakhi closely. 'Really, Pakhi, there's no end to your fecundity. Now you're on the eighth. But pay close attention to me. This time I'm not going to vacate the outhouse for you.'

She finally understood what *Amma* had meant when she had stepped into her outhouse yesterday and exclaimed in delight, 'Oh, so you've fixed this side room. It can serve a purpose in time of need.' Now Pakhi's condition had clearly shown the need. Put up the barricades, she thought, otherwise you'll be driven from here as well. At that very moment *Bade Bhaiyya* materialized from somewhere.

'No reason for you to worry, Munni *beta*,' he said. 'The visionaries will populate new communities.'

'How is that, *Bade Bhaiyya* . . .?'

'We're off to Phoolbari. Enough of this place, now the village world will make our acquaintance.' *Bade Bhaiyya* announced his decision with composure.

Amma and *Baba* were disturbed at the very thought. 'Where are you going to, sir? Is that any place to live in! It'll have a bad effect on the children's studies. There's not even a proper school there.'

'What are you saying, *Baba*? There are not one but two high schools there, one for the girls and another for the boys.'

'But, son, the medium of instruction there is Bangla, and that way we'll lose our . . .'

'So what, *Baba*? If we have to live here, we have to mingle with this soil. This will strengthen our roots,' *Bade Bhaiyya* interrupted *Baba*.

'You may think that, son. My experience is that grafting ourselves on this soil will not make a difference. A graft will always be seen for what it is.'

'No, *Baba*. Your attitude is wrong. You can think this way,' *Choke Bhaiyya* intervened. He was visiting Santahar from Dhaka. This was around 1958 or 1959 when arrests were taking place very quietly and he had thought it best to come home with the least amount of fuss. The family would be pleased and at the same time the danger would be averted. Now here he was arguing with *Baba* with the greatest of ease.

'Has anyone been able to place controls on thinking, sir? If that had been possible would I not have moulded you, who are bent on reducing our traditions to dust, to my way of thinking? Our coming generations will not even know . . .'

'You have no right to say that, *Baba*. We did not express any desire to come here, it was your decision. It was you who rebelled against your traditions – now which traditions are you talking about? You tore a sturdy tree up by its roots and tried to transplant it in this soil: why are you now fed up with this world?'

'Why I'm fed up is my personal business. As far as coming here is concerned, I never made a wiser decision in my life. It is my belief that we will never receive salvation in the next world if the children's future has not been secured. And, son, all of you can see that you have not been losers in this respect. The self-confidence that you find within yourself, and the determination to get your point of view across, is the gift of freedom, a gift of this free society. To be free in name alone is no freedom, sir. Turn to your past. In the city you left behind, you will find your own brothers, listless and, despite their abilities, cowering in their shells . . . and then look at all of you, making such fine progress according to your individual talents.'

'You are under a misapprehension. In this time of alienation we cannot speak openly and you . . . you think this is true freedom?' *Choke Bhaiyya* spoke bitterly. 'This military rule, what's your opinion of it?'

'Who has told you that it is brave or clever to support this regime? Why don't you just take over the business of state? Who has stopped all of you?' *Baba* was a government servant and not prepared to hear a word against the government of the day.

'What wonderful things you say, *Baba*! That would be like snatching sugar cane from an elephant. Is all this possible in a system where free speech has been silenced?'

'It is best that you keep out of the debate of what is possible and what is not possible by keeping quiet. It is best for all of us this way,' *Baba* said sternly.

'Even if we silence ourselves, don't you think others will raise their voices about these timely issues? I believe that even if our lips were to be sealed the very walls would speak.'

'But I say you should hold your tongue. Are you getting ready to go back to jail?' *Amma* looked at *Choke Bhaiyya* in terror.

'As far as jail goes, *Amma*, people are being picked up every day. Only yesterday they took Pakhi's brother away. Yesterday it was his, today it may be our turn. In these times whoever has the courage to speak the truth will suffer the fate of Mansoor al-Hallaj.'

'There's no need. I don't want a Mansoor or a Messiah. Look how you've disgraced me, you wretch. No one has ever been to jail in my family. As for Pakhi's brother, who can say anything about him, he seems to take pleasure in getting himself handcuffed. Where we come from, only hooligans and vagabonds go to jail.' Like a typical mother-in-law, Mother lacerated the festering boils.

'Excuse me, *Amma ji*,' Pakhi opened her mouth in front of *Amma* for the first time. 'Maybe where you come from they are hooligans and vagabonds. Here things are quite different. It is only we, who even when handcuffed, dare to speak the truth. Fear the moment when the fury of the storm will blow away everything with it.' After all, *Amma* had, in an extravagant statement, turned her brothers, who were reputable political workers, into hooligans and vagabonds.

'Pakhi dear, are you any less than a storm yourself? See how you are sweeping all that we love along with you.' Understanding the delicacy of the moment, she had attempted to restore good humour to the conversation.

For the moment the matter was defused and in a few days *Bade Bhaiyya* packed his belongings and went off to celebrate his new life in the outback. After his departure *Amma* began to lose interest in the house which would still resound with their voices. Baby and Rani had matriculated. *Baba* could have sent her off to the hostel, but to send all three was beyond his means, so he thought it best to gather all of them and move to Dhaka.

It was probably around 1960 or 1961 that she graduated from college to enter university. She discovered that *Choke Bhaiyya*, still considered a child by Baba, was quite an important person in the university world. His ideological positions and individual way of looking at things had endeared him to all. In those days, nobody bothered who was an original resident and who was not. People were just concerned with the taste of the fruit, nobody was interested in counting the trees.

While studying in college she had felt that the roots of hatred had weakened considerably and had lost the capacity to flourish. The joy of life itself, the striving after truth and mutual trust and confidence would uproot it for ever. She was convinced that as time went by, if right thinking prevailed, the positive values of life would be strengthened and the difference between resident and non-resident would disappear. The example of *Choke Bhaiyya* was before her. *Choke Bhaiyya* didn't know Bangla well, as Urdu was his mother tongue, but, to share with others the voice of his conscience, he would speak broken Bangla and English and he was not discriminated against but loved by all. When she joined the university *Choke Bhaiyya* had already left but the consciousness created by him, his words, his passion, was still alive in his followers. In all matters he was considered a friend of the underdog. In the most difficult conditions, whenever there was a ray of hope, people had complete faith in *Choke Bhaiyya*. The walls of hatred are falling down, she thought happily.

People were naturally drawing closer to each other and she who had felt self-conscious speaking Bangla in front of Pakhi was now speaking it with ease, however incorrect and broken. When *Bade Bhaiyya* came to Dhaka on *Amma*'s death she saw that the extremely smart and easy-going *Bade Bhaiyya* had disappeared. He who had been famous in the family for being well-dressed in the latest fashions was now, in the style of the quintessential Bengali butcher, attired in loose trousers, sported flowing locks and spoke Urdu in halting tones. This was the *Bade Bhaiyya* for whom *Amma* had renounced life – her only regret on her death bed was that Bengal had swallowed up both her sons. One had been so mesmerized by the Bengali magic and absorbed in his family that he had forgotten that he was part of another family as well. The other was so fond of disentangling the tangled locks of Bengal that six months out of the year would be spent in jail. So *Amma* was among those fortunate ones who had all the luxuries in the world, but her sons turned out to be rebels and it was not in her fate to be blessed with even a few drops of water from their hands as she lay dying.

When she died, *Bade Bhaiyya*, whose elegant Urdu and perfect pronunciation had been held up as a model by his teachers, was now, with complete ease and no embarrassment, confusing the masculine and feminine genders and talking to his children in fluent Bangla, for was that not his children's mother tongue? He had in all matters erased his identity and sought to merge himself with this land. What is all this and why is it so . . . why Bangla? Why can't we get to the root of the matter, she would think; and unintentionally talk to Pakhi and the children in broken Bangla and the children would smile, wondering why their aunt could not speak properly. Pakhi would burst into laughter and say, 'Leave it. Why should you speak Bangla? I'll talk to you in Urdu.'

She was astonished to see that Pakhi's pronunciation in Urdu was now better than *Bade Bhaiyya*'s. When she expressed her surprise, Pakhi had smiled and said, 'Why not? This is the language of my children's father.' Seeing Pakhi's good humour and pleasing conversation, she felt the need to go and spend some time at *Bade Bhaiyya*'s home. It was a strange coincidence that whenever *Amma* had gone to Phoolbari she had been unable to accompany her. Sometimes she would have her exams or then Rani would, and sometimes there would be no one to take care of *Choke Bhaiyya* and *Baba*. Now was the perfect time.

With *Amma* gone, *Baba* suddenly realized that Rani and Baby were adults. Placing them in the care of *Choke Bhaiyya*, he got ready to go to Phoolbari with *Bade Bhaiyya*. This time there was no reason for her to stay on in Dhaka since she had passed her M.A. and was waiting to find a job. She wanted to go to Phoolbari anyway. Whenever Baby and Rani had returned from there, they had brought back the fragrance of *motia* and tales of Pakhi's good humour and *Bade Bhaiyya*'s affluence, and for weeks they would be regaled with stories of *Bade Bhaiyya*'s comfortable and happy existence. The picture they would paint, from the *hilsa* fish cooking in Pakhi's kitchen and the opening buds of *motia* in her courtyard to the children's chatter, made her long to go there. Flowers were her weakness, especially *bela* flowers, and *Bade Bhaiyya*'s obsession with gardening fanned her interest still further.

Listening to these stories, she remembered the time before their move to Dhaka when they had lived in Patna and along with *Bade Bhaiyya* she had planted *bela* flowers in their spacious courtyard. Deep in the recesses of her memory, the day stood out when *Bade*

Bhaiyya had brought the *bela* saplings from school. How carefully the ground had been prepared, the pebbles separated from the earth, and when even that had failed to satisfy, it had been sifted through the sieve kept for cleaning sand. And this was how, in the full heat of the monsoon sun, dripping with sweat, the *bela* saplings had been planted and received their first watering. The plants took to the soil, little buds developed and when one day a tiny flower emerged from the pistachio bush, her small heart had thumped violently in its enclosed space. When she had told *Bade Bhaiyya* the news his face had lit up. It had been a moment of never-to-be-forgotten happiness. That night the plants had yielded huge baskets full of flowers in their imagination and as they talked her eyes kept returning to the bushes in the courtyard. She felt waves of fragrance arising from the solitary flower and engulfing her tiny being until finally, in this heady state, sleep claimed her. The next day she had awoken to find the three doors leading to the courtyard closed and the noise of a great commotion coming from without.

She caught hold of *Choke Bhaiyya*. 'What's the matter?'

'That's where the marriage party will set off,' he said in flat tones, and moved on, balancing his books.

As their house was the largest in the neighbourhood, every other day a marriage party would descend on them. She thought nothing of it as the marriage party came and left, but alas, it carried away the fragrance of flowers with it. Not only had the wretched neighbours entertained the marriage party there, but dug up the entire place so that food could be cooked there to fill the gaping hell of their guests' bellies. The courtyard itself presented the picture of an inferno. All the plants had first shrivelled and then died. She had cried her heart out. *Bade Bhaiyya*, too, had looked sad but as he was older, and a man besides, he had put a better face on it. She had, however, kicked up such a rumpus that, finally losing her patience, *Amma* had given her a few quick slaps.

Bade Bhaiyya had comforted her. 'Let it be, Munni, child. I'll plant a whole garden of *bela* for you.'

The incident blew over. The house and that entire world changed at the same time. What to say of a whole garden of *bela,* when no one had the time to plant a single sapling? In Phoolbari she saw that while *Bade Bhaiyya* had not planted a separate garden, the whole courtyard was abloom, and among the fragrance of the flowers and the sounds of children's voices he was leading a very contented life. Living with *Bade Bhaiyya*, she herself lost awareness that things were changing and that the gathering wings of the storm that Pakhi had so unconsciously feared in Santahar were upon them.

In her last days at university she had sensed that the gulf had widened instead of narrowing. The waves of the Sarjoo were sweeping away the good times. The fire and passion in *Choke Bhaiyya*, whose character and actions had been a source of hope for people, had been extinguished. Despite his best efforts, relationships were ending. People were scattering. Suspicion and mistrust were creating cracks in the edifice of mutual confidence and certainty. The earlier love was now a mere legend, a time when hearts and minds were one and on the face of this earth there was only one right and one left.

Then, as time passed, the headiness of power brought changes in common objectives and paths began to diverge. She began to feel as if someone was poisoning the atmosphere and the flow of running water was being deliberately impeded and channelled in another direction. But water is water and will find its own way. She saw in its surge countless rivulets branching out. Its strong flow, which was once heading in its fullness towards truth, light and life, was dividing, dwindling, stagnating into a slush that over time would breed maggots. So people were corrupted. Obstacles were put in the way. Greed dimmed the vision and the dream.

Living in *Bade Bhaiyya*'s world of fragrant flowers and joyous children, she had forgotten to guard against the evil eye that destroys happiness. Flowers die and their fragrance dissipates in the air. Yes, it had been a mistake to forget.

Evil overpowered good. The enemy attacked with full force and man lost his humanity. Fire devoured *Bade Bhaiyya*'s garden. Pakhi, hair in disarray and fluttering like a thirsty bird, clung to each person in an attempt to save her home. When she herself regained consciousness, the garden had been reduced to ashes. She sought to find herself in that pile of ashes. She looked into *Bade Bhaiyya*'s open, lifeless eyes, eyes that carried pride of life and the light of confident and certain love till the very end. The eyes that had erased their own identity in the dream of a brighter tomorrow were open in amazement now. She looked at *Baba*, who had sought his salvation in a future for his children and who had prayed at *Amma*'s death to be spared a burial in this land as he had watched, in pain, her body float in waist-high water in the grave. Watching his companion's body being reduced to these straits had brought this prayer from the depths of his heart, and because it had come from the depths of his heart God had accepted his prayer. His body was free even of the prison of a shroud. Pakhi's beauty had been reduced to ashes. Her tiny, unopened buds had been consumed by the flames. And she . . . she herself lacked the strength to die, so she had drunk the poison of life.

Translated by Samina Rahman

Khalida Husain

Hoops of Fire

So one by one the four of us embrace Salima. We shed the requisite amount of sympathetic tears; we draw on experience and hearsay to tell her true stories and countless tales of other happenings, crises and catastrophes.

'I'd warned you,' says Rafat, in her usual manner.

'You could see it in his face, damn him', . . . says Zakia, examining her face in her pocket mirror. 'Yes, send him to hell, it's hardly worth ruining your good looks by weeping over him. Have you been using that moisturizer, by the way? Your skin looks so dry . . .'

'Don't talk such rubbish', Rabia snaps. 'What we ought to be thinking about is a course of action. Yes, a plan . . .'

Action! And what can you expect to do now, now that it's all over, when it's already happened – when it keeps on happening, will continue to happen, it's been going on since the beginning of time, will probably go on for ever . . .

God, what fools you are.

I don't bother to speak. I watch the weeping Salima, her torrents of tears, I am absorbed in my envy of her good fortune. Such a display of grief, so direct, so simple, in these times of ours, so much agony and all because she's been abandoned. So women still possess such treasures of tears, of emotions?

A ring of bright blue and yellow lights, of seething, screaming lava, revolves in my head, like those hoops of fire you see in circuses, which people – or dogs – leap through to the spectators' wild applause, while useless, hypocritical, cowardly beings like me keep wondering what they feel.

I shudder. A noose tightens about my neck. Enough.

I consider complimenting Salima on her treasure of tears, but I settle for silence. So you really suffer so deeply, and all because a man has abandoned you? And you, too, will you leap through hoops of fire, and ask for applause, while hypocrites like me keep on wondering what you really feel?

'Listen, you do know Farida, don't you? Now we know what happened to her. All those years go by and then X turns up and tells her his sole intellectual rapport in the world is with her, and she does have half a dozen children to console her and brighten her life. After all, he has a wife who makes those divine rice dishes.' Zakia is still trying to console Salima.

'Yes, and you know that Farida's recently set up an association? Hmm, she keeps asking me to join her, too.'

'Association?' Stifling a yawn, I finally speak.

'Yes, to get rid of the plague of intelligent, aware women in our society. She thinks that if some girl shows contagious symptoms of an overdeveloped intellect, she ought to be married off when she's barely reached puberty so that she can produce lots of healthy babies at the perfect age, fulfil her destiny, take her place in the scheme of things, dress up in pretty clothes and chant songs of praise for the Prophet in the company of women for the rest of her life . . .'

A faint smile plays on Salima's lips. She retrieves a fragile scented handkerchief from her elegant handbag and raises it to her eyes. 'Marvellous!' Rafat is delighted to see Salima smiling. 'Take me, I've got two daughters, if I don't get them married off by the time they're sixteen you can change my name. I've even made a vow . . .'

'What? And when did you become religious?' Rabia is apprehensive.

'No great harm in making a vow, is there? If your prayers are granted, you pay up, well and good, and if not what do you lose?'

'Just look at all of you, merrily chattering away because you can afford to. You have homes, husbands, children, there's a sense of great purpose in your lives, but what about me? – I'm so attractive and still I'm stuck in a lonely, gloomy room surrounded only by pictures. I have to kill time, kill life, murder it, I'd say . . .'

'Don't go away, Salima, sit down, you're living in a world of dreams. You know what they say about distant drums . . . it's hardly the paradise you make out, you know, married life, I mean. When two people live together . . .'

The cue for a gale of laughter from Rabia. 'Yes, what you need for those special moments are your deodorants, radiant teeth, fresh and fragrant breath, bright eyes, and what really happens is that after a few weeks . . .' Her words dissolve in another fit of giggles.

'Oh, for God's sake, Rabia . . .'

'Well, I'm right after all: after a few weeks a demon called togetherness creeps up to strangle you, erases your identity, and you forget those bacteria-killing toothpastes, you think that spending money on scent is an atrocious waste, and then comes the grand revelation, the man beside you sweats so heavily . . .'

'Oh, do shut up, Rabia.' Rafat restrains her mirth.

'But in spite of all that, you don't have to kill your time staring at silent, lifeless pictures. And . . . and . . .' Salima stops in mid-sentence.

We dispose of our half-full cups of tea, prepare to disband. It occurs to me, for a moment, to stop Salima, to take her with me, but I restrain myself because the world is so full of noise that I can't hear a word, and if I could I wouldn't understand. Salima, I recognize that place where you're stranded, I know it so well, you're like a part of myself that's been released from the prison of the present moment. That loneliness of which you speak can also be a haven. You've laid down your weapons too soon. Solitude is protective, pacifying, a mother's bosom. It's the loneliness beyond that never ends, is limitless, the twilight region of time that spreads and enfolds everything, that each of us has to face alone, yes, each one, in the midst of silent, lifeless pictures or in the shadow of vital, fortunate others.

The loneliness of that place is relentless – it tells you for the first time that you only belong to yourself because you're separate from everyone else, you are yourself only because the other is separate from you. And that is why, every hour and every moment, you try to close those gaps and distances between yourself and the other, you're lost in the music of harmony and union, but the music and the ecstatic bond are equally unattainable. And knowing this is like turning your face away from happiness.

I pick up my handbag and leave. Perhaps we're all sent here on a mission of penance, which we pursue without end. And still we know that we haven't paid the price of our gains or of our losses. It keeps on rising. God spare us. Again the flame flares in my head, circling, revolving, rising, spreading. I have to leap through it, in this carnival emptied of entertainers. An act I have to perform alone, with no one to watch or applaud me, no one to bear witness. But without this flaring flame I have no existence, I am a non-presence, that's the sum of the story: from the circling, soaring, searing flame I came to know that I am; and I exist because on the face of the volcano my name is inscribed.

I am seated in front of the doctor with thick white hair, soft voice and gentle hands. On the table between us, a miscellany of x-ray photographs and medical reports.

'Everything seems to be fine here, Mrs . . . There' s nothing wrong with you.'

'I knew that I was perfectly well, Doctor . . .'

'Well, then – you're a well-educated lady,' he says, softly. Yes, Sir, I'm an educated ignorant lady, so my healers say – (well, then, lady, if you're alive, she must have been dead for over a hundred years) – an ignorant educated lady of the sort that this society churns out by the day – that's the diagnosis, at least.

'Listen, if you don't have any real worries of your own, then you could do worse than thinking about the state of the nation, do some charity work, worry a little less about your children and get involved with a cause instead. But first of all you have to stop thinking about yourself. Look at the wretched of the earth – you could always join a religious circle, find yourself a guru, a spiritual guide . . .'

'Thank you, thank you very much . . .' I gather up the mass of papers, stand up and leave. A guru, a guide – you make me laugh. I am one myself.

Then I think of Tehsina. Once when we met, years ago, she'd said, looking, as usual, at some distant point over my shoulder, 'What, after all, is the root of your problem? Bread? Clothes? A roof over your head?'

Those healthy problems, I thought, that make you human and clothe you in flesh, that tie you to the ground and keep you alive, a living, breathing organism, that change you from a shadow, a husk, into a thing of weight, those matters that change the map of the world.

'What *is* your problem, then?' Tehsina was persistent. 'Just being?'

It's beyond your comprehension, Tehsina, a matter – for once! – that you can't understand. Non-existence, negation within negation. A vision, perhaps, that I alone among my loved ones can see, which, against my will, I can't share with them, because it appears in its own solitude, the solitude that is the destiny of us all, which was given to my parents and their parents and their progenitors, on and on since the first man, before the beginning of time. We have to confront it. We must.

Alone.

'Well, then,' Tehsina said, annoyed by my silence, 'what I've heard is true – you've developed a retrograde sensibility, you've become superstitious, decadent and pessimistic. I suggest you start to think about the Third World and connect yourself with all the backward, deprived, sick nations; that way you can still redeem yourself.' She gathered up her bundle of books and took off.

Third World – and am I not answerable to that world, beyond the Third World, that lives within me? Answerable to a wasteland of anguish and sorrow, for my cry, 'I am here!', is imprisoned in my ribcage. I have to leap into the soaring flame, though I have no witness.

And now, tonight, it lies before me. I rise from my bed; it lies in wait for me.

'What is it, what's the matter?' Arif asks, taking my icy hand. 'You're seeing things. Fantasizing. Hallucinating.'

'No. It's not a hallucination – just stay by me. I have to leap in.' I hang on to his hand. And mountains, like balls of cotton, fly on the wind, and the earth spills forth its hidden treasures, and the gates of the seven heavens are thrown open, and then the fiery hoop of burning colours appears, rising, spreading, hissing, spitting sparks, and I become a moth and dance around it, around the erupting volcano I sway, for I have reached my destination, for all time, for ever. And I am not afraid, for the fire is my destiny – look, I dance with dread and hope, with hope and dread I await the moment when the flame must submit to become my saviour.

Translated by Aamer Hussein

Glossary

Abba, Baba	Daddy
Amma, Ammi	Mummy
apa	older sister
Arrey!, Arri!	exclamation roughly equivalent to 'Hey!'
bahu	daughter-in-law
Bari Ma	Granny, lit. 'big mother'
Begum	lady; Madam. Originally referred to a noblewoman but now formally used as an equivalent of Mrs
bela	variety of jasmine
beta	child, lit. son
Bhagwan	God (Hindu)
bhai	brother; *Bhaiyya, Bade Bhaiyya* (big brother) and *Choke Bhaiyya* (little brother) are affectionately respectful terms for an older brother
Bibi	lady; Miss
bidi	local cigarette
bindiya	spot painted on forehead
bitiya	diminutive of *beti*, daughter
burqa	long-hooded robe, often black, worn by women who observe strict religious codes of dress

chappati	pancake – like unleavened bread
charas	a drug
dai	midwife
Diwali	Hindu religious festival of lights
dulha	bridegroom; *Dulha Bhai*: affectionate term for brother-in-law
dupatta	scarf-like garment worn by Muslim and other women for modesty or as adornment
Eid	Muslim festival
ektara	one-stringed musical instrument
ghee	clarified butter
godown	warehouse
gurdvara	Sikh place of worship
Hai nee!	Punjabi exclamation
hari (m.), *hariani* (f.)	Sindhi agricultural worker
harsinghar (also *sheoli*)	jasmine
haveli	traditional mansion
hilsa	variety of fish
jaman	fruit of jujube tree
ji (e.g. *Amma ji*)	suffix indicating respect
kafir	infidel
kaka	Punjabi nickname for the son of the family
Khuda hafiz	Goodbye
kulfi	pudding akin to ice cream
mama	mother's brother
mlech	Hindu term for an outcast, particularly a non-Hindu
motia	variety of jasmine
munni, munni rani	little one, little queen; nicknames for girl children
mushaira	assembly of poets
neem	lime
paisa	coin and monetary unit equal to one-hundredth of a rupee

pakora	savoury fritter made of chickpea flower, often eaten as a snack with tea
peepal	type of tree
pulao	rice dish
raja	ruler
Ramayan or *Ramayana*	the epic legend of the Hindu god-king Rama and his consort Sita
rani	ruler's wife; queen
sadhu	holy man; mendicant
Sahib, Sahiba	honorifics roughly corresponding to Sir and Madam
salaam	greetings, obeisance
samosa	triangular pastry filled with minced meat or vegetables
seer	varying unit of weight (approx. 1 kg)
shalwar	loose, baggy trousers
sheesham	type of tree
Shrimati	Hindi/Indian equivalent of Mrs
takht	divan
tonga-walla	driver of a *tonga*, or horse-drawn carriage
tum-tum	horse-drawn carriage
yaar	mate; pal
zamindar	feudal landlord

Biographical Notes

AZRA ABBAS was born in Kanpur, India, in 1950, and migrated as a child to Karachi, where she has lived ever since. One of the best known of the new wave of feminist poets, she has published some short fiction as well as an impressionistic memoir of her childhood, *Mera Bachpan*, translated into English as *Kicking Up Dust* by Samina Rahman. Abbas is a teacher.

RAZIA FASIH AHMED was born in 1926 in Muradabad, India, and migrated to Pakistan at partition. Best known as a prolific novelist, she rose to prominence in the mid-1960s with a prizewinning novel, *Abla-pa* [Footsore]. She is a fine experimental short-story writer and has published *The Man in the Mask*, a volume of her own work, in English.

ALTAF FATIMA was born in 1929 in Lucknow, India, and migrated to Pakistan at partition. A teacher of Urdu literature by profession, she has published several collections of short stories and novels, the best-known of which, *Dastak Na Do*, has been translated by Rukhsana Ahmad as *The One Who Did Not Ask* (1993). Fatima lives in Lahore.

JAMILA HASHMI was born in eastern Punjab in 1929. An acclaimed prizewinning novelist, she rose to fame in the 1960s with a series of long and short novels, including the prize-winning *Talash i Baharan* [The Search for Spring], which deal with the lives of Sikhs and Hindus as well as Muslims. In the 1980s she published novels based on the lives of the famous Bahai prophetess Qurratulain Tahira and (her most highly rated work) of Mansour al-Hallaj. She died in 1988.

KHALIDA HUSAIN was born in Faisalabad in 1938. One of Urdu's leading short-story writers, she has been compared to Virginia Woolf and Kafka among others, but is more influenced by classic Sufi texts and excels in reworking traditional forms. The author of several acclaimed collections of stories, including *Pehchaan* [Recognition] and *Masruf Aurat* [The Busy Woman], she is now working on a novel and a collection of essays. She lives and teaches in Islamabad.

HIJAB IMTIAZ ALI was born in 1903 in Hyderabad, India, and grew up in Madras. The daughter of a novelist, she began to write at an early age, influenced by French romanticism and Turkish fiction. In the 1930s, already a famous writer, she took a pilot's licence, becoming the first Indian woman to fly a plane. She married the writer Imtiaz Ali Taj – the son of Urdu literature's first major female figure, Muhammadi Begum – and moved to Lahore, where she has lived ever since. She has published works in all literary genres, the most renowned of which are the novella *Meri Natamaam Muhabbat* [My Incomplete Love] and the Freudian novel *Andhere Khwab* [Dark Dreams]. Her reputation as a pioneering prose stylist has recently been revived with the republication of her work in Pakistan.

FARKHANDA LODHI was born in Multan in 1938. She has written several volumes of short stories and a highly acclaimed novel, *Hasrat-i-Arz-i-Tamanna* [Unfulfilled, Unspoken Yearnings]. She writes in Urdu and Punjabi. She lives in Lahore, where she is chief librarian at Government College.

KHADIJA MASTOOR was born in 1927. She migrated to Pakistan from her native Lucknow after partition. An active member of the Progressive Writers Association, she held strong left-wing and feminist views which colour her fiction. Primarily a short-story writer, she is nevertheless best known for *Angan* [Courtyard], the first of her two feminist novels, which covers the years before and after the independence of India. She died in her early fifties, in 1982.

FAHMIDA RIAZ was born in Karachi in 1945 and grew up in Hyderabad, Sind. Her first volume of poems was published in 1965 and she has subsequently published several others. An outspoken radical and feminist, she spent several years as a refugee in India during the military regime of General Zia, but now lives and works in Karachi, where she runs a feminist press. An acclaimed Urdu poet, she has emerged, with the novel *Godavari* and the long narrative *Karachi*, as one of the most innovative and original contemporary prose stylists in Pakistan, combining techniques of documentary with fiction in her work.

MUMTAZ SHIRIN was born in Bangalore, India, in 1924. One of the most influential Pakistani critics of her day, she wrote widely about the effects of partition and the new nationalisms on Urdu literature and introduced the idea of the *nouveau roman* and other postmodern techniques to Urdu fiction. Her essays are collected in two volumes, one of which focuses on the writings of the famous writer Manto. Shirin published only two collections of short fiction. She died in 1971.

UMME UMARA lived in Bangladesh, then East Pakistan, until its war of liberation in 1971. She then, like many Urdu speakers, migrated to what is now Pakistan. Somewhat underrated as a writer, she has published several collections of short fiction and a novel.

Notes on Translators

YASMIN HAMEED is associated with education. She has published several volumes of poetry in Urdu and a book of translations, *The Blue Flower*, in English. She is the co-editor of a special issue on women's writing of the journal *Pakistani Literature*.

SHAHRUKH HUSAIN was born and brought up in Karachi, Pakistan. Originally a scholar of modern Urdu poetry, she wrote the Urdu screenplay of Ismail Merchant's *In Custody*, based on Anita Desai's English version. The author of several books for adults and children, notably *Women Who Wear the Breeches* and *Temptresses: The Virago Book of Evil Women*, she is now a practising psychotherapist and writes and broadcasts on feminist and cultural issues. She lives in London.

AAMER HUSSEIN *(editor and translator)* was born and brought up in Karachi, Pakistan. He has lived in England since 1970. Best known for his collection of stories, *Mirror to the Sun*, he has written for the *Times Literary Supplement*, the *Times Higher Education Supplement*, *The Independent*, *The New Statesman* and the *Literary Review*. One of the leading critics of Urdu/Pakistani literature in the West, he contributed the title story to *Fires in an Autumn Garden*, a volume to mark the fiftieth anniversary of the creation of Pakistan, and in 1996 lectured in Pakistan's three major cities as a guest of the Pakistan Academy of Literature. He has taught Urdu at the Language Centre of London University's School of Oriental and African Studies, post-colonial literatures at Queen Mary and Westfield College, Westfield, and now lectures on South Asian studies at Pepperdine University, London.

SAMINA RAHMAN was born in Aligarh. She now lives in Lahore, where she is principal of the LGS College for Women. Her publications include *Pre-Mughal India*, *The Education Jungle* and *In Her Own Write*, a collection of stories in translation.

ATIYA SHAH is an educationist who specializes in the teaching of English.

14.95